Now Do You Get It?

Stuart Newton

authorHOUSE®

AuthorHouse™ UK Ltd.
500 Avebury Boulevard
Central Milton Keynes, MK9 2BE
www.authorhouse.co.uk
Phone: 08001974150

First published by AuthorHouse 2/4/2010

ISBN: 978-1-4490-8162-1 (sc)

This book is printed on acid-free paper.

Contents

PREFACE

The themes of this book are naïve and simplistic!

They are based on the ideas that:

(a) democracy in UK has been corrupted by many politicians who have lost touch with the people they represent, through arrogance, misplaced loyalties, evasiveness and, in some cases) dishonesty.

(b) 'ordinary people' (like you and me) can make a difference to the situation.

There are plenty of erudite textbooks on political structures, political processes and political philosophy. They have their place, but I find some of them very heavy-going: they are rather like those cryptic crosswords where I don't understand the question, even when I know what the answer is supposed to be!

In the end, politics is for people. Politics exists to improve the quality of life of all of the citizens.

It does not always feel like that to those of us who are on the receiving end!

We must not let democracy in the UK fall apart because MPs and voters have lost contact with each other.

If we are to re-engage a majority of UK citizens with our

democracy, then we must change the way in which we do politics in UK. More specifically, we must change the way in which politicians do politics in UK.

It is simple.

It is naïve.

The academics and the politicians will laugh.

The rest of us will probably scream if we continue to be marginalized by the political process in UK.

We need to take the opportunity of the expenses scandal to make it clear to MPs that their lives have changed………. for ever.

Stuart Newton

Brighton

March 2010

13 Principles to improve our Democracy

This book is written with these principles in mind:

A. 'Ordinary' people can make a difference.
B. Each of us must vote.
C. People around the world are dying in the fight for democracy: in the UK democracy is allowed to die, because people cannot be bothered to fight for it.
D. Democracy is too important to leave in the hands of politicians.
E. The expenses scandal has undermined the democratic process in UK, because now voters distrust MPs even more than they did before.
F. A healthy democracy encourages active participation of all of the people.
G. The loyalties of a Member of Parliament are, in order of priority, to:
   a. constituents,
   b. Parliament,
   c. political party.
H. MPs have a duty to consult regularly with their constituents, of all political persuasions.
I. All voters have a duty to ensure that our elected representatives cannot easily ignore us again.
J. MPs work for voters and, therefore, voters must have significant representation in discussions of the roles and remuneration of MPs.

K. One of the roles of the new generation of MPs is to clean-up Parliament.
L. Most voters in UK are angered by the usual strategy of "Yah-Boo" politics.
M. The expenses scandal is not a party-political issue: the abuse has involved members of all parties.

Chapter 1 THINGS MUST CHANGE

This book is written out of sheer anger and frustration.

There will be a General Election in UK on, or before, 3 June 2010.

We, the voters of UK will have to choose people to represent us in Parliament. This is one of the few occasions when 'ordinary' people are called upon to do something democratic.

And yet the present generation of MPs have provided us with few, if any, reasons to trust them. Like it, or not, very many of us believe that if there is a conflict between the interests of voters and party, it will be the party that will be supported by an MP. We also believe that there are very many MPs who will use public funds, without shame, to finance a lifestyle that is not available to the large majority of taxpayers.

And, as if that were not enough, supporters of our political parties really do give the impression that it is personal **power** that is important, rather than **service to people**. It may be that those party-members do not realise the impression that they give, or perhaps they don't care. But, let us be clear, the **only** reason for the existence of any politicians and the political party of which (s)he is a member, is to improve the quality of life of **all** people.

I can't think of any politician who makes that point clearly, and passionately, and with conviction. Can you?

In 2010, many of us are deeply cynical about the value of any of our political parties. Just look at these (heavily-edited) comments from blogs in some of our national newspapers. They were collected in May 2008, a year before the expenses scandal broke. The theme of the blogs was the growing level of violence on the streets of Britain, and there were many hundreds of comments about what should be done. A number of those comments expressed anger and frustration with a political system that seemed unable or unwilling to respond to the needs of ordinary people. It is useful to remind ourselves that these comments were written one year before the expenses scandal hit the headlines.

(a) People make up the country. We need to talk, to brain storm ideas and to put them into action. To tackle a problem we need to consult people who are directly involved. We should not wait for some hero to arrive at the door with superpowers to fix it: if you don't take action locally, nothing will change.

(b) We are bleating about how bad things are. Does anyone have any ideas how to make them better?

(c) Let's vote to take action. If enough people registered an interest then we could organise a rally. A mass demonstration of 1 or 2 million people could bring UK to a standstill. It won't happen because the majority of people in this country just sit on their backsides and do nothing but moan.

(d) Make sure that people vote. The trouble is that all

we ever do in this country is a lot of whingeing, so I can't imagine people doing anything as exhausting as getting up and voting. To get anywhere people need to be active.....

(e) What about the next stage?.....The Labour government is unwilling to listen to us or fix the problems, and the Conservatives before them were the ones who created the problem. So who will make the necessary changes? If we don't sort that out then this whole discussion is just a lot of meaningless words.

(f) Reform the electoral system so that 'ordinary' people are not totally disaffected by decision making which is irrelevant to their own circumstances.

(g) We get cheesed off with all the lies and all the pocket lining that goes on. What about a party that actually does what it promises?

(h) Sack all MP's and let some of us here do the job, bring some democracy and real people into the decision making processes of the UK.

(i) We need to vote not only on change of Government but accountability of Government. If they are caught telling porkies to the nation, that's _fraud_. If they are caught saying one thing and doing another, that's _deception with intent to commit fraud_. Is it not time that Ministers and other MPs were held accountable for their decisions, and their mistakes?

(j) All parties must work together – after all there is little difference between them.

(k) This situation will continue unless people say 'no more'. Politicians rely on our apathy and ignorance. We have to change the system for the good of us and our children. Nothing will change otherwise....it's that simple!!!

(l) If we all wrote to our MP, or visited her/him at the surgery, perhaps (s)he will take note but, if all we do is write on forums, then we are no better then the people who sit on their backsides and do nothing at all.

There is real passion here. But no action seems to have been taken.

It is disappointing that few, if any, of these comments have been acted upon by the elected politicians, and few, if any, of these comments have been taken up by the various newspapers concerned. Disappointing, but probably not surprising. An MP has 60 000 or more constituents, and national newspapers count their readers in millions, so who cares if a few hundred bloggers let off steam?

It is disappointing that few, if any, of these comments have been acted upon by us, the voters.

This book is to ask how we can change this situation: after all, it's not as though this issue is a new one.

Concerns about the personal integrity of MPs were around long before the expenses scandal broke early in 2009. For instance, in a poll conducted by YouGov (February 2008), respondents were asked to agree or disagree with this statement:

'Most MPs use public office to make money improperly'.

79% of people agreed with the statement.

Just remember, this was **one year** before the expenses scandal hit the headlines!

For far too long our MPs have been held in almost universal contempt by the electorate: and they have done nothing effective about it. Here are just two stinging comments from the media (2008) that sum up that contempt:

"Do any MPs recognise or, worse still, care that they are held in contempt by the majority of the voters?"

"MPs of all parties surely must be aware of the contempt which most normal people have for them."

Whose fault is that?

MPs have only themselves to blame. Sleaze at Westminster hit the headlines in the eighties and nineties. As a result, politicians spoke many fine words about cleaning it up. If anything, it has got worse.

And the problem is not merely about sleaze. Politicians in this country have had an appallingly bad press for as long as most of us can remember. Many voters believe that MPs have no concept of what life is like for 'ordinary' people in UK, and many of us regard MPs with little or no respect. And yet again, in spite of all that has been said and written, they seem to have done little to alter the public perception that they are arrogant, self-serving and two-faced.

And, just when we thought that it could not get worse, it did. In 2009, the expenses scandal broke, and all of our barely-hidden fears about the duplicity and sheer mind-boggling arrogance of MPs were exposed. The careers of some of them went in to freefall, and just a few emerged unscathed.

The large majority of us find it hard to comprehend that MPs can justify creating an expenses system for themselves that enables them to claim (from the taxpayer), payments in excess of the average annual wage in UK. It makes things even worse when they do it at a time of economic meltdown: it verges on the obscene that they do it at a time when a very large percentage of 'ordinary' people in UK are struggling to make ends meet. It is deeply disturbing that some MPs from all parties have treated the expenses system as a way of getting extra cash.

It's nice work if you can get it.

Clearly, there are many MPs, in all parties, who have behaved with impeccable integrity. It is unfortunate that they have been branded as dishonest and lacking in principles or understanding, because many of their colleagues have been caught with their hands in the till. But, that's life. It might have helped if some of those undoubted pillars of integrity had spoken out against an iniquitous expenses system that was kept secret from the people who had to pay for it.

It could be that, in another time, at another place, there

would have been less anger for MPs who were merely following the rules. But it isn't another time, and it isn't another place. We are talking about UK 2009, and the decades of Westminster sleaze that preceded it. This was the year when the expenses scandal was exposed. It was the straw that broke the camel's back.

It is a time when ordinary families have to make economies on essentials such as food and heat. It is a time when pensioners are struggling to survive on the state pension. And yet many MPs bill the taxpayer for £100 worth of food a week, for 52 weeks a year. They seem to have no sense of shame that they are claiming more money per week for eating than many pensioners receive from the state to pay **all** of their living expenses.

It's a time when workers who ask their bosses for a pay rise are likely to be laughed out of court. The response is likely to be along the lines "You are lucky to have a job at all, mate" or "If you think you are worth more, go and get a job somewhere else." And yet, many MPs are seriously pushing for a substantial payrise for themselves – and the odds are that they will get it.

It is a time when soldiers risking their lives in war zones do not get sufficient high-quality equipment or, it seems, sufficient equipment of any quality. And yet, many MPs have milked the system to get state-of-the-art high-tech equipment for their homes. Who pays for these luxury items? It is the soldiers, and all of the other taxpayers in UK.

It is a time when the only way to get staff into NHS hospitals is to bring in workers from abroad, because so few people in UK are prepared to undergo the lengthy training, work the long hours, expose themselves to unpleasant infections and dirty conditions for……. peanuts. It is ironic that many MPs seem to justify their own salary plus expenses with an argument such as: "If the state won't pay a decent wage, then we won't be able to recruit good quality people to be MPs." It's a pity that the argument for getting high-quality MPs does not seem to apply to getting high-quality nurses (and teachers, and police officers and social workers etc).

Very soon, our present MPs, or those who wish to replace them, will come to us pleading for our votes. The question is whether we shall let those MPs, or the parties that they represent, off the hook. Will we assume that they have learned their lesson after the battering that they received in 2009?

The answer is, of course, that we should not assume anything of the sort. How do we find out if MPs **have** got the message? Well, we could do the same as is required of schools. If teachers need to find out whether children have learned important knowledge and skills, a test is provided. Those students who have conscientiously and effectively learned the relevant knowledge and concepts score high marks. Those students who have not learned them effectively achieve poor marks, and must try again. We could use a similar strategy with MPs, after all they approved the system of regular, frequent testing for children, so they cannot, with integrity, complain if they have the same treatment, can they?

Of course, the cynical responses are: "Yes, they can complain.", and "Who said anything about integrity?"

Later in the book (pages 64-5) there is a list of questions that we could give to all Parliamentary candidates in each constituency. Each candidate would be required to submit answers, and these would be published in local newspapers. In this way, voters could obtain some useful comparative information that we could use to help us make a rational choice between the candidates available.

Sadly, it is quite obvious that some MPs have NOT learned their lesson. Some refuse to admit that they have done anything wrong in making outrageous expense claims, and fall back on the tired old excuse that "It was all within the rules". Some of these individuals refuse to reimburse anything to the taxpayer. On the other hand, some have decided to pay-up. Perhaps, they have had severe pangs of conscience, and sleepless nights as they regret their duplicity. Or, perhaps they have worked out that they will lose votes if they do not return what was, morally, not theirs to have in the first place.

But, apart from greed, MPs must take responsibility for another serious betrayal of voters. Many (probably a majority) of them are no longer trusted by the voters. This undermines the whole concept of democracy in Britain, and may go some way to explain the dreadful turnout statistics for our national and local elections.

Abraham Lincoln famously said in the Gettysberg address (1863),

> *"Democracy is government of the people, by the people, for the people."*

No MP, as far as I know, has ever denied the wisdom of President Lincoln's words, so let us assume that they all accept the statement as an accurate and perceptive summary of an idea that is fundamental to our way of life in UK.

"Democracy is government **OF** the people…"

Yes, that bit applies: we certainly are on the receiving end of a lot of government.

"Democracy is government….**BY** the people…."

It ought to be true, but many MPs have demonstrated that as soon as they leave the world of real people, and get into the rarefied atmosphere of Westminster, they lose contact with that reality, and stick their snouts in the trough along with the others. Parliamentary candidates may make promises to real people in the run-up to the election, but far too many of those candidates seem to forget their obligations to voters once they arrive in the corridors of power, and automatically transfer their loyalties to the Party.

"Democracy is government……**FOR** the people."

At the sharp end, it just doesn't feel like that – especially when we are expected to fork out vast amounts of extra cash to fund a lifestyle for MPs that seems to suggest that they think of themselves as being on a higher plane than the rest of us.

The expenses scandal is one more nail in the coffin of democracy in UK. One of the outcomes is that many of us do not trust our representatives to represent us. We do not believe that they are either able or willing to understand, far less to share, the hardship that so many people in UK are facing. Twenty years ago, we found little evidence of their empathy with voters: that quality seems even less apparent in 2010. The outcome of this dreadful state of affairs is that an increasing number of people have given up voting in recent years: more are threatening not to do so in 2010.

That undermines democracy in UK.

Our crooked MPs have a lot to answer for.

You will find nothing in this book that supports a particular party but you WILL find a message here that says that, in the run-up to the General Election of 2010, we must give the Parliamentary candidates of all parties a drubbing that they will never forget. If an individual cannot behave with personal integrity, or (s)he represents a party whose members cannot behave with personal integrity, then can we expect either the individual, or her/his party, to represent our country with integrity? MPs need, and deserve, a very hard time, to ensure that they get the message that we will not tolerate this abuse of our democracy.

You will also find a frequent message that says: "Please, please, please VOTE in the General Election".

This time round, we should make sure that MPs have to earn their title "Honourable Member". That will not happen if they regain their Parliamentary seat simply because not enough people voted for anyone else.

This book suggests some of the practical things that we can do to make that happen in 2010.

It suggests what we must do **before** the date of General Election is announced.

It suggests what we must do **during** the General Election campaign

It suggests what we need to do **after** the General Election is over.

Doing nothing is, of course, the easy option.

That is the strategy supported by those who refuse to vote.

It is also the strategy that our current herd of MPs know and love – it gives them a comparatively quiet life.

Our tasks are to:

(a) persuade everyone to vote;

(b) give Parliamentary candidates an exceptionally hard time;

(c) hold our new MPs to account, and ensure that they give value for money;

(d) build a system of democracy that will be worth having, and will be a lasting legacy for future generations.

That's what this book is about.

Chapter 2 BELL (tower), DUCK (house) and (s)CANDLE WHERE DID IT ALL GO WRONG?

This chapter looks at the background to some of our difficulties in 2010.

There are three key, and frequently repeated, ideas in this chapter:

> *(a) Democracy is too important to leave in the hands of politicians;*
> *(b) 'Ordinary' people can make a difference;*
> *(c) Each of us must vote.*

Democracy in Britain has been compromised by too many dishonest MPs

This chapter is long. Its purpose is to remind all of us just how disgracefully some of our MPs have behaved. The chapter focuses on the expenses scandal, as well as the lack of trust that so many of us feel towards our representatives. The expenses scandal merely brought things to a head. After decades of political sleaze, over-bearing arrogance, and inadequate representation of voters by many MPs, we could be forgiven for hoping that they might be motivated to do something effective to repair the damage and restore their credibility.

It hasn't happened.

This is part of a letter that I sent to the Daily Mail on 15 September 2006.

> *Who is worried by the public's perception that MPs lack integrity?*
>
> *Clearly not the MPs.*
>
> *We have told them for years that we do not trust them. Their response is to look serious, wring their hands, and do nothing.*
>
> *Duplicity is one of those issues that has all-party support – there are too many who seem to have no problems with being less than honest with voters.*
>
> *It's just the voters who dislike it - and they don't count.*
>
> *Newspapers have voiced public outrage about political lying and half-truth for the last twenty years. Unfortunately, MPs know that all the outraged public ever do is moan and whinge.*
>
> *And nothing ever changes.*

The problem of inappropriate behaviour by our MPs goes back even further. Nearly 40% of British people who were eligible to vote in 2001 and 2005 didn't actually do so. The turnout figures for 2001 were the worst in a British General Election since 1918.

But even those figures look good when you compare them with turnouts for the election of other politicians, such as local councillors, or for Members of the European

Parliament: in some areas of Britain the campaigns for those elections did not generate enough excitement to interest even 20% of the voters.

Why did two out of five people not vote in the last two General Elections? Some of the non-voters recently gave their reasons:

> *"There is so much information out there, but no way of deciding what is true... The fact is that people do not believe politicians."*

> *"When I am trying to understand what a party is offering all I get is one party 'slagging-off' the other parties!"*

> *"I don't vote. I have all of the information I need, and I have discovered that nobody represents my views."*

> *"It wasn't lack of information that stopped me voting it was the fact that it was all the same. There is very little that is different between the current political party manifestoes."*

Such comments are serious indictments of our politicians. The candidates and the party-faithful may enjoy the adrenaline-rush and amusement of party-political games, such as the deliberate ploy of giving evasive answers to straightforward questions, slagging-off opponents, and pretending to an omniscience that is far from true. But, for the rest of us, those games are part of the problem - they are pathetic, childish and largely irrelevant to the needs of voters.

At every election in recent memory, voters have complained that they do not like 'Yah-Boo' politics. In their turn, senior politicians have assured us that they do not like such tactics either, and that they will not allow it to happen in the future. But, unfortunately, whether we like it or not, that's what we get. For instance, today, 6 January 2010, probably 4 months before the General Election, they are already at it. Prominent politicians are engaged in telling us what is wrong with other parties, rather than sticking to a clear and unambiguous statement of the policies of their own party. They say that they want to stick to the issues, and then launch into a slanging match. The insults are devised to cloud the issues, and are about as edifying and useful as witnessing gangs of kids squaring up to each other in a playground fight. When the issues are as fundamental as choosing who will govern us for the next four or five years, and ensuring that the process is raised out of the normal gutter of political 'debate', then it is little wonder that politicians are not trusted. The simple fact is that senior politicians are unable or unwilling to honour their words, and are not up to the task of controlling their subordinates. Why should we believe that they will be successful in running the country.

The comments above, from voters disillusioned with our political system, come from the heart of the writers. Clearly, they are not the messages that MPs and their cronies want to hear. This is because most politicians:

(a) do not know how to do democracy in ways that are different to the usual circus of slanging-matches, back-stabbing and half-truth;

(b) know that to find a solution to the concerns of voters is likely to restrict their activities and, possibly, their lifestyle, and

(c) have never done politics by listening to ordinary people, and then taking decisive action on behalf of those people.

All the indicators are that voters are now even more cynical about politicians than they were thirty years ago. The comments on blogsites in 2009 suggested that the turnout for the 2010 General Election will be even worse than in the last two. For instance, in the summer of 2009, just after the expenses scandal hit the headlines, thousands of bloggers vented their wrath on the dishonesty of MPs: these two comments sum up the general feeling:

"Whatever the consequences, I will never vote again."

"MPs think that they can con us into voting for them again – well, I won't."

When more revelations came in December 2009, yet more angry words were written – here is a quietly passionate, and deeply sad, remark from one disillusioned voter:

"I have always voted before, because brave men and women have fought and died in World Wars to defend that right for me, but I will <u>not</u> vote in 2010."

Many cynics sum up their feelings with the words:

"Will the last one to leave Britain please turn out the lights."

It is outrageous that the greed of a bunch of hypocritical MPs should have persuaded ordinary people to give up on the UK's version of democracy.

Our elected representatives have seriously undermined our democracy. In former times that would have been regarded as a treasonable offence. Today, in laidback UK, the question is whether we care enough to get off our backsides and DO something.

PEOPLE AROUND THE WORLD ARE DYING IN THE FIGHT FOR DEMOCRACY. IN UK DEMOCRACY IS ALLOWED TO DIE, BECAUSE PEOPLE CAN'T BE BOTHERED TO FIGHT FOR IT.

There are plenty of countries around the world where 'ordinary' people, like you and me, have died and are dying, in the struggle for democracy. There are too many countries in the world where power-hungry nutters have elections, but only accept the results if they win. Whatever the outcome of their version of democracy, those despots continue doing just what they intended to do in the first place, irrespective of the wishes of the voters.

But, here's an irony. When politicians in some of those countries have been dragged, kicking and screaming, into some semblance of democratic election, the UN sends in observers to check that things are done correctly. The team of observers often includes people from our country. For instance, in 2009, observers from UK went to Kyrgyzstan, Moldova, Uzbekistan and Croatia to check the validity of their democratic procedures during national elections. Perhaps UN should send external observers from other countries to check on the democratic procedures that we have in UK. Why? Not because of problems with the administration of the actual vote, (with very rare exceptions, the outcome of UK elections seems to reflect the number of votes cast by the voters who made the effort to take part). No, the UK (the country with the oldest democracy in the world) probably needs external observers to assess the extent to which the disengagement between voters and their representatives is undermining our democratic processes.

The behaviour of some of our MPs has managed to destroy the trust and honour that is fundamental to any democracy. Those MPs have a lot to answer for.

Just a reminder of those inspiring words of Lincoln, already quoted in chapter 1 – 'Democracy is government **of** the people, **by** the people, **for** the people': those words are just as relevant to us in 2010 as they were in 1863.

Those words ought to inspire, in each of us, a belief in the fundamental principle of democracy. It is this:

'ORDINARY' PEOPLE CAN MAKE A DIFFERENCE

If 'ordinary' voters in a democratic country cannot make a difference to our system of democracy, then what is the point of being a voter? Indeed, what is the point of democracy?

The loudest answers to these questions will come from the millions of people who do not have the privilege of living in a democracy.

And yet, in Britain, and possibly in other so-called democracies, our answers to those questions are so quiet that outsiders may not be able to hear them. We act as though we are ashamed of living in a democracy. We act as though we believe that there is nothing that an individual can do. We act as though we believe that 'ordinary' people cannot make a difference.

In Britain, our representatives may do things in a more subtle way than some of the world's thuggish dictators – but the lust for power is alive and well amongst some of those at Westminster. Some of them really do seem to believe that they were born to power and, of course, its associated perks. In order to satisfy that lust for power, many of them will do whatever is necessary. They will promise the earth when they want our votes, and yet have no problems with ratting on those promises when they have been elected. Once we have given them our votes, they will go and act exclusively in their own interests and those of their parties. Whether they intended to or not, the clear message that many of those MPs regularly give to us is: "To hell with the voters." It is immaterial whether they deny such an accusation. The behaviour of so many of them speaks far more eloquently than their words. It is the perception of many voters that MPs regard us as irrelevant.

The only surprise is that, in a free democratic country, we allow them to get away with such crass duplicity election after election.

It is time for our party system to have a massive shake-up – from the voters.

Will it happen?

It certainly will NOT happen if voters choose to 'punish' their MPs by refusing to vote. Indeed, one of the most powerful 'punishments' that voters can give to our politicians is to make sure that we definitely **do** vote: it is the **only** way in which change will happen.

EACH OF US MUST VOTE

It is important to remind ourselves of the cause of our current problems.

It is this. We, the voters, have allowed our democratically-elected representatives to get out of control. We have allowed our representatives to make up their own rules, with no input from, and no control by, those who elected them.

That was a stupid mistake.

That control has to be regained by us, and we will not do that by refusing to vote.

If 'punishment' is to be our strategy, then its most effective form will be to give all Parliamentary candidates an exceptionally hard time in the run-up to the election, and then to use our votes.

There is an important underlying idea here. It is one that each of us should remember – every day. It is also an idea that every Parliamentary candidate needs to repeat twenty times before (s)he goes to bed, and thirty times before (s)he gets started on the work of a new day:

DEMOCRACY IS TOO IMPORTANT TO LEAVE IN THE HANDS OF POLITICIANS.

Voters in Britain are disengaged from the political process

In 2004, the Power Commission was set up, independently funded by the Rowntree foundation, to investigate the fundamental disengagement between voters and Parliament in UK. Their report, published in 2007, was called 'Power to the People'. During their deliberations, they received written submissions from many members of the public, and called on oral evidence from a number of experts. One of the issues that they investigated was the changes that would have to take place in order to re-engage people with the democratic process in UK.

In their conclusions, the Commissioners mention possible reasons for voter disengagement. They felt that these suggestions, from UK voters, were supported by the evidence that had been collected from other sources:

Citizens do not feel that the processes of formal democracy offer them enough influence over political decisions – this includes party members who feel they have no say in policy-making and are increasingly disaffected.

The main political parties are widely perceived to be too similar and lacking in principle.

The electoral system is widely perceived as leading to unequal and wasted votes.

Political parties and elections require citizens to commit to too broad a range of policies.

It is discouraging that politicians appear to have done absolutely nothing to change those perceptions. If they had made an obvious attempt to address some of them, then that might have gone some way to re-engaging voters with our democracy, and to improving the personal standing of some politicians. The lethargy on the part of MPs does not provide convincing evidence that there is a political will to improve the system. Indeed it endorses one of the hardest-hitting comments in the Report:

> *"We were struck by the strength of the contempt felt towards formal politics."*

This really MUST change.

One of the general Conclusions of the Power Commission is this:

> *"The outcome of inaction will only be ever greater decline in the public esteem in which politicians are held. Ultimately, it is possible that the brief local upsurges in support for anti-democratic and populist parties and candidates will develop into local, regional and even national mutinies as popular disenchantment with the main parties, elections and political decision-making is mobilised and focused.*
>
> *The potential for this to happen would be magnified vastly should Britain suffer a period of economic slowdown in the future. It would be foolish to underestimate the campaign value to an extremist party or candidate of combining popular economic alienation with the widespread political alienation...."*

These words were written in 2007, but provide a prophetic

glimpse of the country as we head towards the General Election of 2010. Clearly, the writing was on the wall in 2007 but, although it was clearly spelled out in the Power Commission's report, nothing has been done to tackle it. It seems as though, in UK, politicians of all parties are content to muddle on, and hope that no disaster happens. This could be an application of the maxim "If it ain't broke, don't fix it." What is the converse of that statement? It ought to be: "If it **is** broke, fix it." But, in Westminster, it seems that the converse is more likely to be: "If it looks as though it **is** broke, it's not really, because that's the way we've always done things around here."

Just read those two paragraphs from the Power Commission once again. It would be very unwise to show our contempt for politicians and our distress with an unhealthy economy by simply not voting, or voting for extremist parties who do not even pretend to believe in democracy.

EACH OF US MUST VOTE

It is depressing, but not surprising, that the findings of this Commission have been quietly shelved. After all, the comments from disillusioned voters are unanswerable, and the recommendations of the Power Commission show a level of wisdom and prophetic insight that do not seem to be readily available in Westminster. Unfortunately those recommendations will demand changes in the way that our MPs do politics. Members of Parliament have not, in the past, been responsive to change that involves their way of life.

And so, the mutual contempt and hostility continues between voters and their MPs.

The findings of the Power Commission do not seem to have motivated anyone to do anything.

Well, have you ever come across an MP who has promised to do something to implement its recommendations?

Have you ever come across an MP who even acknowledges the existence of the report from the Power Commission?

Have you found any reference to the Power Commission in a newspaper, or on the radio or on television?

Have you come across any report by a journalist that has used the findings of the Power Commission to hammer greedy MPs?

Even worse, have you actually HEARD of the Power Commission?

Of course, if the Commission had included some comments about axing "I'm a Celebrity, get me out of here" then we would all have heard about it. Summaries of the Report would have hit the headlines every day for months. There would be full-page articles about its findings, and gloomy forecasts about the end of civilisation as we know it.

But that's not what the Commission did. They just talked about boring old democracy, and who cares about that in UK?

Evidently not the voters.

Evidently not the media.

Evidently not the politicians.

Democracy in UK is floundering because of two particular problems: (1) not many voters are interested in the views of politicians, and (2) not many politicians are interested in the views of voters. That's a pretty scary scenario, because it indicates that many of our MPs and the parties to which they belong have, effectively, lost contact with real people.

And, far from feeling guilty and trying to improve their credibility in the eyes of the voters, many MPs have actually achieved the amazingly difficult task of reducing their moral authority even further.

Clearly, that cannot go on. Change is necessary.

And ours is the generation that must do it.

The following words (usually attributed to Margaret Mead) put the idea so powerfully:

"Never doubt that a small group of committed people can change the world. Indeed, it is the only thing that ever has."

In rather less enduring words:

'ORDINARY' PEOPLE CAN MAKE A DIFFERENCE

Indeed, we must start making a difference, because no-one in power seems to be ready, willing or able to do so.

Specifically, in Spring 2010, that means that we, the 'ordinary' voters of democratic UK can, and must, make a difference to our future. The General Election of 2010 should be a clear example of British bloody-mindedness in action.

It should be a year when MPs learn the hard way that voters can call the shots as well.

2010 is the year when:

EACH OF US MUST VOTE

That, in itself, would be one of the biggest wake-up calls for Parliament in its history.

Look out! It's payback time!

Are we prepared to give this warning to our Parliamentary candidates?

The evidence for the general contempt in which MPs are held has usually been in the form of gut feelings rather than hard facts and figures. At least, that was the case until April 2009, when the expenses scandal broke, and the hard evidence was handed to us on a plate.

It appeared, from the evidence that, out of the 646 MPs, about 30 had been involved in activities that might reasonably be described as fraud.

A much larger number had clearly stretched the extendable rules on expenses to the very limits of their elasticity.

They may not have broken the letter of the law, but they had certainly been creative in interpreting its spirit – and, in the process, they were guilty of betrayal.

That mass of data clearly demonstrated that our democratic system had been comprehensively screwed by a sizeable number of greedy MPs. These people have claimed massive, and unjustifiable expenses, at a time when the majority of voters are suffering serious financial hardship. Their greed has:

- **betrayed their voters,**
- **betrayed their parties,**
- **betrayed their many honest colleagues, and**
- **betrayed the idea of Parliamentary democracy in Britain.**

Most of us were appalled by the abuses of the expenses system but, in retrospect, we should not have been. Any reasonable person might have worked out that if MPs were allowed to devise a system of expenses for themselves that enables them to milk the taxpayers (under a cloak of secrecy), then many would have been too spineless to resist the temptation to abuse it.

In the months following the publication of their outrageous expenses claims, voters became incandescent, and the credibility of MPs fell to an all-time low. The word 'contempt' does not even begin to describe the views of the voters with regard to very many MPs.

The response of MPs and party leaders has been the equivalent of re-arranging deckchairs on the Titanic.

In spite of everything that has been written and spoken, many MPs still come up with the excuses "But I haven't done anything wrong", or "I was just following the rules" (that is, the rules that they formulated, and ratified, and attempted to hide from public eyes).

Many of them still cannot grasp the idea that supplementing their salaries in this way is over-indulgent and underhand.

Many MPs really cannot understand why taxpayers felt betrayed and angry when we discovered that we were paying for MPs to indulge in a lavish lifestyle, at a time when the majority of the people of UK were struggling with rising prices and job insecurity. [There were, of course, a few MPs who did understand that we might be angry – some of these were the MPs who tried to keep the whole affair secret.]

If they really were surprised that voters were angry with them, it might have been wise if they had asked us about it. It would have been good if some of those MPs had found the courage to ask you and me why our perceptions of their actions were so different to their own. Perhaps then they could have asked us how they could repair the damage.

Well, perhaps some MPs asked you for advice.

Or perhaps they asked members of their families.

Or perhaps they only asked their chums.

Or perhaps they didn't ask anyone, because they did not want to know the answers.

We have allowed the British version of democracy to be quietly corrupted by those who should be its champions - our Members of Parliament.

In spite of all that has been said and written, many STILL don't get it. And they still do not understand that things have to change. That change involves the voters. Let's hold on to that view:

'ORDINARY' PEOPLE CAN MAKE A DIFFERENCE

We elect them and we pay them to represent us. We should expect them to be accountable to us. But we have let them off the hook, so it's not surprising that they get out of control, in their own private club, with its arcane rules, and unearned privileges. All the signs are that they will do it again if given half a chance. And that is not going to happen, is it? Why? Because in a democracy:

'ORDINARY' PEOPLE CAN MAKE A DIFFERENCE

Don't merely dismiss the idea as simplistic and naïve. Probably the only reason that 'ordinary' people do not usually make a difference in a complex world is that we have never tried.

We may, of course, dismiss the idea that you and I can make a difference, because it is too difficult.

It may be that we dismiss the idea because we don't much care what Parliament does, so long as it does not mess with 'The X-Factor' or shut the pubs. If we really are as shallow as that, then we deserve everything we get.

Right now, the democratic system in UK has been compromised. It's about time that we sorted it out, if only to make it healthy for our kids. Young people do not deserve the legacy of our complacency. If we pass on to our children the present unhealthy and tainted UK system of democracy, then they have every right to ask us why we did nothing, especially at a time when our MPs were on the skids. Our responses to that question are likely to be along the old traditional lines: "You don't understand. There's nothing that one person can do." And we can fall back on blaming everyone else for not being courageous enough to stand up and be counted.

Do those excuses sound convincing to you? Our kids will not be taken in by them.

If we are not going to sell our children short, then it's time we got up and did something useful. Isn't it?

Of course, that's not about storming Parliament, or manning the barricades. But it IS about making our presence felt, and our views known.

So, in 2010 the messages that we should be giving to our MPs, and to those who are trying to become our MPs, are these:

We are fed-up with being screwed by our MPs.

We will no longer tolerate the hypocrisy, the platitudes, the underhand dealings and the selfishness.

We are fed up with political posturing.

We are fed-up with comments such as: "We are all in this together.", when manifestly that has not been true of our MPs for years.

We are fed up with comments about the need to 'tighten our belts' and 'act with restraint' in making pay claims. [Statements such as those merely succeed in making most of us feel sick, when we discover that such restraint and belt-tightening applies to everybody in the country, except MPs.]

We shall want some much harder evidence than mere words before we begin to believe that any politician has earned our trust, and is worth listening to. Only when we have that evidence might we be persuaded to vote for her/him.

That's the powerful message that we need to give.And, right now, they don't get it.

What's more, they don't get it that they don't get it!

If this system is going to change, then we, the voters have to make it change.

That means you and me.

We, the voters, have taken a backseat with regard to democracy, and we have left it in the hands of our representatives. Some of them have managed to comprehensively screw it up. They have demonstrated very clearly the truth that:

DEMOCRACY IS TOO IMPORTANT TO LEAVE IN THE HANDS OF POLITICIANS.

It's not rocket science. If we are not happy with the way things are going in this country, then we need to do something to change it. And, what better time to do it than in the run-up to a General Election?

MPs know that they can rely on most voters in UK to shout a lot when they are angry, and then to do nothing useful. They know that we really do believe that 'ordinary' people cannot do anything to change our democratic system. Many MPs are hoping that, by the time that the election date is announced, we will have forgotten their shady acts, their dodgy expenses claims, and their pathetic attempts at self-justification.

Some MPs have developed an argument that could be described as the skin-care offensive. The argument goes along the lines that they should have more money:

"Because we're worth it".

Yes, the argument is surreal.

It would even be funny, if it wasn't so pathetic, misguided and totally inappropriate given the economic climate in UK at the moment.

As it is, unlike a skin-care product with a similar name, this one has a nasty smell.

There are some honest MPs around

In the last year, pretty well all MPs have been labelled as corrupt and contemptible. Of course, that is an unfair judgement on the many excellent MPs in the Commons. Those MPs represent their constituents with honesty, compassion, humility, strength and straightforwardness. MPs like these are often the ones who make themselves unpopular with their parties. They won't be pushed around and frightened into toeing the party line. They are willing to put the interests of voters before those of the party. I guess that many of those MPs are well-known, in their constituencies and beyond, as people who are passionate about their job, and totally committed to the people that they represent. They are the ones who give us hope for the future of Parliament. It's unfortunate that these first-rate MPs have been unjustifiably tainted by the expenses scandal.

Sadly, some of those honest MPs decided long ago that they would retire from Westminster at this election: it's a pity, because we need them now, as never before.

We really ought to remind ourselves of the integrity of these people, because some bloggers suggest that they have all been at it: "Snouts in the trough", "Idiots", "Traitors", "Morons", "Fraudsters, thieves and liars" are just some of the printable comments, made about ALL MPs, by some angry bloggers! It is not surprising that these descriptions were followed up with suggested punishments – such as deselection, arrest, criminal proceedings, and a host of much more painful (and terminal) procedures.

But, that's the way life is. Because there is a sizeable chunk of dishonest and useless MPs, all of them get labelled as dishonest and useless. It's like that for the rest of us as well. MPs spend much of their time drafting and passing Bills that restrict the activities of everyone, because there is a small percentage of crooks in our society.

But there is a worrying downside to acknowledging the fact that there are many honest MPs. It is hard to believe that so many claim not to have known that the expenses system was being abused. Was this ignorance genuine, or is the truth that no-one **wanted** to know what was going on? It may be that some MPs wander about at Westminster with their heads in the clouds and really do not know what is going on. It may be that others are too spineless to expose a system that cheats the taxpayers. These qualities are neither admirable nor useful for dealing with the harsh realities of life that face most 'ordinary' people in UK of 21st century.

It's worthwhile remembering that MPs passed a law in 1999, specifically to help people who perceived an injustice at work, and who needed support in exposing it. This is often called the Whistleblowing law (actually its real name is the Public Interest Disclosure Act 1998), and a large majority of the present bunch were MPs in 1999 when it came into force. It's sad that not one of those very honest and upright MPs felt sufficiently courageous to support the voters, and use the Whistleblower's Law to expose the outrageous claims of some of their colleagues.

Of course it may be that private conversations did take place between honest MPs and those with their fingers in the till. Perhaps an honest MP expressed disgust with the other's abuses of a system paid for by the long-suffering taxpayer. It would be good to have evidence of such conversations, since it would demonstrate that there was some spine somewhere in Westminster.

Whatever the truth, we have to remember that we are now approaching a General Election. When you and I next hear a gang of MPs in the House of Commons, sneering and jeering at their opponents, we might remember that they only seem to be courageous when they are in a pack made up of members of their own party. In that situation they are confident enough to indulge in the Westminster version of democracy in action. These are the people who represent UK on the national and international stages. These are the people who express their outrage at the abuses of democracy in other countries. These are also the people who are only courageous in a gang, and some of them use subterfuge in order to line their own pockets.

Wrestling with your conscience

In fact, the real courage in the expenses scandal was demonstrated by one or two civil servants and private individuals who put their futures on the line for this story. It takes a very special sort of courage for one or two individuals to decide to take on the whole of the political establishment. Lesser men and women would have chickened out.

Just think about what it involved. Early in 2009 the expense claims of MPs were being collated in the Fees Office in Westminster. Someone in that office was appalled.

Like you and me (s)he had watched TV coverage of the repatriation of the bodies of soldiers killed in action in Iraq and Afghanistan.

Like you and me (s)he had heard stories that soldiers were poorly equipped to deal with enemy-fire.

(S)he had heard that some soldiers had saved some of their meagre wages, so that when they were on leave in England, they could try to buy better-quality body protection for use when they were returned to the front line.

And then, (s)he read the details of the outrageous expenses claims of MPs – the one group of people in the country who were actually in a position to make the lives of soldiers better, and safer. But, instead, they seemed to be more concerned about obtaining plasma-screen TVs, up-market furniture, and duckhouses – at taxpayers' expense (and those taxpayers, of course, included serving soldiers).

Those selfish individuals fed their faces on £400 worth of food a month (the budget allocated to feed three, four, five or six frontline soldiers) – all at taxpayers' expense. And, possibly the ultimate insult, one MP even charged taxpayers for buying a wreath to lay at a Remembrance Day commemoration – that must have gone down well with soldiers serving in the frontline.

When that courageous civil servant decided to expose this extravagance, the information was passed to someone else who took the decision to get those details published. He was putting his future freedom on the line – for a principle that is vital to our democracy.

Then there were the members of staff at The Daily Telegraph - a very British institution. But, powerful as it is, the editor and his staff knew, better than most, just what could be the fall-out from publishing details of these outrageous expense claims – but they still went ahead.

It's a courageous act to take on the most powerful people in the land, and I guess that the individuals who leaked the expenses information, and the journalists who investigated it and wrote about it, had plenty of sleepless nights as they contemplated what could happen to them. But, they did it, because they believed that we, the taxpayers, had a right to know. Those few courageous individuals put their livelihoods and liberty on the line so that we could learn about the hypocrisy and mendacity of a substantial number of our Members of Parliament.

So the rest of us had better start doing something more effective than talking.

We owe those civil servants and journalists an immense debt of gratitude and admiration for their courage.

Would the rest of us have had his courage? Or would we have fallen back on the age-old excuse "No-one likes a snitch"?

Would any MP, in similar circumstances, have had the courage to say: "This is wrong", and stick to her/his principles, whatever the consequences? Self-evidently, none of them were brave enough to do so, otherwise the expenses scandal would have been exposed years ago.

If you or I were in the position of the civil servant who exposed the scandal, we would probably have said: "It's wrong, but there is nothing that one person can do."

That sort of comment is an excuse for laziness or cowardice. Most of us do not do anything, not because we **cannot** do anything, but because we **cannot be bothered** to do anything.

In the end, that brave individual wrestled with her/his conscience, and her/his conscience won.

What would have happened if (s)he had wrestled with her/his conscience and the conscience had lost the battle?

What would have happened if (s)he had chickened out, believing that (s)he would have become the target of the intense anger of the Establishment, the local politicians, and the media?

What would have happened if (s)he really could not be bothered with all of the hassle that it would have caused?

If (s)he had done nothing, then what would have happened? Well….nothing.

MPs would have been a whole lot happier than they are now.

And we would have been none the wiser about the secret code of immorality indulged in by too many of them, which allows them to misappropriate our money without any sense of guilt.

The bad news for the complacent majority in Britain is that now we DO know.

Now it's **our** time for action.

That's what you and I have to do now.

It won't require too much courage: after all, the tough stuff has been done for us already. All we have to do is act together, because the fundamental rule in our democracy is that

'ORDINARY' PEOPLE CAN MAKE A DIFFERENCE

If we cannot take that on board, and act on it, then the massive upheaval caused by the Daily Telegraph's revelations about MPs' expenses will have been a waste of time, and we will have betrayed the immense courage of the people who broke the story.

The result of all of that courage is a story for UK that must not die.

It was Thomas Jefferson who once remarked:

"Where the government fears the people, there is liberty. Where the people fear the government, there is tyranny."

He does not seem to have envisaged a situation where there is mutual contempt. Still, that unfortunate aspect of Britain's political life can become history – if we are prepared to make it so. Today, we should be aiming for Jefferson's definition of liberty.

The exposure of the duplicity of some MPs could not have come at a better time – just a year before a General Election. No wonder that politicians are listening. No wonder that they are worried. No wonder that many of them are leaving politics. If you and I, the voters of UK, cannot scare them witless this time round, then we really have lost it. It is our chance to ensure that:

'ORDINARY' PEOPLE CAN AND MUST
MAKE A DIFFERENCE

Can MPs rely on voters to have forgotten the whole incident before the General Election of 2010?

Are MPs already confident that, in spite of acres of newspaper coverage in May and June 2009 we will have forgiven their dishonesty with comments such as "Everyone fiddles their expenses"?

Do MPs believe that most of us are bored with the story, and believe that it's time to move on? Do they know that we switch channels if the story comes up on television?

Are British voters living up to the expectations of politicians: we are all talk and no muscle? We talk a good game – just so long as no-one expects us to **do** anything.

Taking action on the abysmal behaviour and attitude of our representatives will not put our future well-being on the line, but it will get over the message to future MPs that their lives have changed forever.

If we play our cards right, there will never be a time in the foreseeable future when we have politicians so comprehensively on the run as they were in 2009, and will be as we approach the General Election of 2010.

If they get away with the usual party-political games in 2010, it will be our fault.

If we can't be bothered to give them a hard time in 2010, don't let us bother to complain that MPs never listen to what the voters want.

They are listening now. Are we doing enough talking? Are we prepared to take enough serious action? We MUST have mechanisms for holding our elected representatives to account. We **<u>must</u>** make democracy work more effectively in UK, and 2010 is the year to do it. Remember:

'ORDINARY' PEOPLE CAN MAKE A DIFFERENCE

DEMOCRACY IS TOO IMPORTANT TO LEAVE IN THE HANDS OF POLITICIANS

EACH OF US MUST VOTE

Chapter 3 'ORDINARY' PEOPLE CAN MAKE A DIFFERENCE

This chapter considers the action that we need to take before the date of the General Election is announced.

There are three key, and frequently repeated, ideas in this chapter:

(a) The loyalties of a Member of Parliament are, in order of priority to

    (i) constituents,

    (ii) Parliament

    (iii) political party.

(b) The expenses scandal is not a party-political issue: the abuse has involved members of all parties.

(c) MPs have a duty to consult regularly with their constituents, of all political persuasions.

At every election in living memory, voters have complained before the campaign, during the campaign and after the campaign. We have complained that too many MPs:

- **have no understanding of the life of most of the people in UK;**
- **place loyalty to party much higher than loyalty to voters;**
- **talk at voters rather than listen to them;**

- appear to be in it for what they can get out of it, not for what they can put in;

- are more interested in trading insults with opponents, than working together to find lasting and workable solutions to the problems that we all face;

- seem to believe that they are something special, rather than our representatives;

- seem to have had a morality by-pass, which enables them to screw the taxpayer without conscience.

Of course, it's not that surprising. Until the mid-1990s in most constituencies MPs have been able to take it for granted that there would be no change in political affiliation. In a large number of constituencies you could put up a chimpanzee in a blue or red scarf and it would win for the appropriate party. After that, a chimpanzee's loyalty may well be influenced not by the people who voted for it, but by the person who distributes the bananas.

That analogy will be regarded as dismissive and insulting to some of our MPs, and yet it does seem to relate to the way in which a substantial minority of them treat the voters. Those MPs need to have an attitude transplant.

It may be necessary for the next lot of MPs to get their heads round the idea that the voters expect to be listened to. MPs who are successful at the next Election will need to demonstrate an ability to respond positively to the demands of voters, rather than merely jumping through the appropriate hoops determined by their parties. In other words:

THE LOYALTIES OF AN MP ARE, IN ORDER OF PRIORITY, TO CONSTITUENTS, PARLIAMENT AND PARTY.

This idea is not new. It is similar to the responsibilities listed in a document from the House of Commons Information Office

The Role of an MP

MPs have responsibilities to three main groups: their constituents, Parliament, and their political party.

One MP is elected to the House of Commons by each of the UK's 600+ constituencies. MP's duties in Parliament include participating in debates and voting on legislation and other matters. They may also be members of committees examining new laws or the work of government departments. Some have a role as a minister in government or a spokesperson in opposition.

MPs can help their constituents by advising on problems (particularly those that arise from the work of government departments), representing the concerns of their constituents in Parliament and acting as a figurehead for the local area.

MPs usually support their party by voting with its leadership in the House of Commons and acting as a representative for the party in their constituency.

This information may come as a surprise to many voters. It may be a surprise to many MPs. Admittedly, the official document does not give a priority rating to the three areas of duty, but at least it lists them in the right order. The question is whether your average MP would describe him/herself primarily as:

(a) "the representative of people in constituency X";

(b) "a representative of Parliamentary democracy in UK", or

(c) "a Labour/Conservative/Liberal Democrat".

Perhaps you should ask the prospective candidates when they turn up in your area.

Get a new life, chum – because the old one is about to change!

So, what must we achieve in the General Election of 2010?

We have to begin to change the way in which politics is done in this country.

Of course, to make effective changes will take some time, and, certainly we shall need a much longer period of time than the few weeks that are left before the Election. There are short-term and long-term tasks. Some long-term ideas are listed in chapter 5, with the suggestion that these, and other, ideas are matters for people to discuss. They involve issues that are far too important for any one individual, such as the author, to declare an opinion as if it were the only possible solution. Indeed, it is for precisely this reason that we have our present unsatisfactory political system. That system is based on the idea that there are just three ways of doing things (Labour, Conservative and Liberal Democrat) and, because those ways have been determined by professional politicians, they must be right. If the voters don't like any of the three packages – tough.

Of course, the reality is that good ideas are generated from groups of people with diverse interests, of different ages, of different backgrounds and with different experiences of life – good ideas certainly do not all come from professional politicians.

We don't choose cars using the 'Three sizes fit all' model.

We don't choose computers, or televisions, or mobile phones, or ovens like that either.

And we should no longer be willing to choose our government like that.

On top of all of that there is the arrogance of each professional politician who believes that the only right way of doing things is the one that has been adopted by her/his own party, and that the alternatives suggested by other parties are nonsense. The politician then adds hypocrisy to her/his list of errors. This happens in cases where her/his own party is now adopting a policy that is contrary to the one that they supported ten years ago. It's encouraging that politicians have the honesty to change their minds. It's disappointing that they do not have the courage to admit that they were wrong, or to apologise for the errors of their party in the past. The time-honoured strategy is simply to rewrite history, deny that anything has changed, and then divert the discussion to the evils of their opponents.

Any MP who seriously believes that the policies of all

other parties are rubbish should get out more. If (s)he did that, and spoke to real people, rather than just her/his cronies, and a group of like-minded members of the public, then those politicians might learn that most of us in the real world don't see it like that.

Few of us want to sign up to (vote for) the total package of measures in any of the three manifestoes. Each set of policies is likely to include some bits that we agree with, some that we disagree with, some that we do not want, some that we do not need, and some that we do not understand. The sooner that professional politicians can get their collective heads around that obvious fact, the better will be their understanding of voters. How will MPs learn that elementary fact of life?

They need to get out of the Westminster bubble and listen to their constituents (of all political persuasions).

They need to use the same state services as the rest of us.

They need to try surviving or working in some of the soulless and desolate estates of UK - day after day after day.

When those events begins to happen, then just possibly we might have policies that mean something to a larger proportion of people.

When MPs have to endure the hardships of real life faced by so many people in UK, then it is likely that real improvements will happen in our state services. Until then, don't hold your breath.

MPs HAVE A DUTY TO CONSULT REGULARLY

WITH THEIR CONSTITUENTS, AND ACT ON THE ADVICE RECEIVED.

In recent years it has been customary for Ministers to announce that UK leads the way across the world in areas such as taxpayer-backed injection of cash to assist banks; housing co-operatives; low carbon emissions; Education Reform (we have, according to MPs, been leading the world in this respect since the 1980s).

Now we, the voters, need to start leading the world in democratic reform. And, God knows, there is plenty of need for that in UK. The important thing to remember is that ordinary people in this country DO want to get involved in changing their world for the better (the Power Commission noted that far more people are involved in voluntary work in their communities than are involved in the party political process). Presumably it is the political processes, and the people who operate them, that is the big turn-off: the recent behaviour of MPs will have done nothing to change that view amongst the electorate.

Year after year, voters complain about being sidelined by politicians. We shout, we write to newspapers, we threaten not to vote, and we do.......damn all.

Things have to change. We will NOT be sidelined. We need to get over the message, time and time again, as loudly and clearly as we can shout it:

THE LOYALTIES OF AN MP ARE, IN ORDER OF PRIORITY, TO CONSTITUENTS, PARLIAMENT AND PARTY.

MPs' expenses – which was the guilty party?

Once the expenses scandal had broken, there were calls for a General Election. This was, of course, little more than an attempt to bring down an unpopular government. And that is not what the expenses issue is about. There are members of all parties who have behaved shamefully and, similarly, there are members of all parties who have behaved impeccably. Any suggestion that the dishonesty is a party political issue is an outrageous attempt at political duplicity. In some ways such a suggestion devalues the information, and the courage of those who broke the story. The man who passed the disk to the staff at The Daily Telegraph, made it clear at the outset that politicians of all parties were involved, and he demanded an undertaking that the journalistic coverage would deal in an even-handed way with all of the miscreants irrespective of their party. This story was far too important to be partisan.

It is surprising that, in spite of the massive amount of documentary evidence available, there are still some people who want to replace fact with fantasy and insist that the expenses scandal resides with one party. The fact is:

THE EXPENSES SCANDAL IS NOT A PARTY-POLITICAL ISSUE: THE ABUSE HAS INVOLVED MEMBERS OF ALL PARTIES.

In May 2009 I wrote to the Editor of a national newspaper that was conducting an online poll amongst its readers on the need for a General Election. Well actually it wasn't a real poll. The question was along the lines of 'Do you think that we ought to have a General Election now?' The voting box provided one possible answer: it was 'Yes'. In this 'survey' it wasn't actually possible to express an alternative view. When a popular national newspaper nakedly biases a 'survey' in this way, is it any wonder that our democracy is on its knees?

The email that I sent by to the Editor is given as Appendix 1.

Perhaps not surprisingly, I did not receive a response!

It was fortunate that the calls for an early General Election were not heeded in May 2009 – because then, the overwhelmingly large majority of the candidates would have been those of the usual parties. A General Election in May 2009 would have lead to many dishonest MPs being re-elected because there was no-one else around to replace them: it is good news for the voters that that did not happen. So, what can we do?

Make a difference by standing as a candidate for election to Parliament!

If we are to change the system for the better, if we are to ensure that 'ordinary' people are represented by those who share their hopes and worries, and if we are to ensure that the loyalty of MPs is to the electorate first, and the party second, then we need a new breed of MPs – actually we need a very large number of them. Many will come from the traditional parties, but it will be good news for Parliament if there are plenty who are independent of the old party system.

You might want to stand as a candidate for one of the

established parties (that's not always easy, because selection often seems to be restricted to those people who have a substantial track record as local councillors or activists).

The other alternative is to stand as an Independent. How realistic is that? Well, in May 2009, polls in the Guardian and ComRes suggested that well over two-thirds of voters would seriously consider voting for an Independent.

What does this mean? 'Ordinary' people like you and me have a fourth choice. In most UK constituencies at General Elections we have to choose between Conservative, Labour and Liberal Democrat, with the possibility of regional parties in Scotland, Wales and Northern Ireland. There is likely to be a host of fringe parties, some of which may campaign on a single issue, and others seem to be there to give colour and entertainment to the process.

In the present House of Commons there are six Independents – two were elected as such, and four have joined them. They tend to have greater clout than many backbenchers, because these people have had the courage and integrity to disagree with conventional parties, either before the last election, or during the present Parliament. For that reason alone, these MPs often have an immense level of affection and respect amongst voters of all parties, in their own constituencies, as well as in other areas of the country.

That sort of strength of purpose, and commitment to people seems to be in short supply in MPs whose primary allegiance is to a political party.

So, would you consider standing for Parliament as an

Independent candidate? If not, would you consider actively supporting someone else who is willing to stand? Would you consider being part of a team prepared to do the necessary spadework over the very short period of time between now and the General Election?

Of course, seeking election as an Independent candidate will be hard work, and demoralising. You will have to endure the sneers and patronising attitudes of the mainstream parties – their line will be that you cannot form a government out of Independents. And that, of course, is true. On the other hand many voters take the line that neither of the two largest parties have been particularly good at forming successful government teams over the last few decades: 'ropey', 'weak', 'divided' and 'disreputable' are some of the least-offensive adjectives that leap to mind.

As an Independent candidate, there is no party machinery to rely on, and you and your team have to make all of the mistakes on the hoof, with no-one to help. There is good news, however. It is this. There is now a new political grouping that provides help and support to Independent candidates – it's called The Jury Team.

We need Independent MPs. They may have a personal manifesto that involves helping to clean up Parliament. They need to be courageous enough to expose the abuses, advertise the inequities and ensure that the Members of the House are reminded constantly that they are there to serve the needs of voters. That's what MPs are for. It's the most important thing that they do. It's also one of the things that many of them do not do well.

If you are thinking about standing as an Independent candidate you might consider the advice given by Martin Bell (a former Independent MP). In his time in the Commons, he was one of the best-known, and most widely-respected, MPs of any party. He suggests that there are three factors that will improve your chances of being elected as an Independent MP: (a) be well known in the area; (b) stand for a good cause, and (c) the current incumbent is unpopular or vulnerable.

If you want to consider being an Independent candidate, contact The Jury Team – soon. Get talking to your friends, because you will need their support. Get talking to the media in your area and, of course, start talking with your family. Are there any people in the area who will provide financial support?

When the date of the election is announced there will be just four weeks for you to get organised – that's not much time to do all that has to be done without a backing party machine – it's one of the reasons the candidates from traditional parties are moderately safe – so few Independents stand because the odds are stacked against people who have to do everything by themselves.

How might we nominate a local Independent candidate? Well we could take the same line as the Conservatives did recently in Totnes. That constituency had to deal with the aftermath of Anthony Steen – remember he was the one who defended his outrageous expenses claims by accusing those who criticised him of…..jealousy! The Tories in Totnes decided to select their new candidate from a shortlist of three approved candidates. All voters in the constituency were eligible to take part in the selection of the Conservative candidate, irrespective of the political affiliation of those voters. The successful person was a GP who has, apparently, had no experience of local or national politics at all. That's a triumph for democracy in UK. This is not, of course, a new system – the Americans call it a Primary, and use it to select Republican and Democratic nominees for the Presidency.

It may be that you are not prepared to stand yourself, but know someone who you trust, and think would do a good job. Your task now is to talk with that person and find out her/his feelings on the matter.

After that, the real work begins. Do other people share your views? Will they support that person's nomination? Will they get involved in the work that is necessary? Will they organise fund-raising?

In areas where the sitting MP has been involved in claiming questionable expenses, the voters are likely to be angry, and the MP may well have an uphill struggle to get re-elected. The traditional parties may all be facing tough times – so there is a much stronger chance in 2010 of Independents achieving a serious percentage of the votes.

The atmosphere at the moment is feverish and unstable. It is being stirred-up by political insult and media-hype. Who knows – an Independent candidate may well win in your area!

Whatever else happens, if you are fed up with the traditional parties and you want an Independent MP, you need to be prepared to support your candidate in what will be a difficult job. You also need to accept that the process will involve a steep learning curve. And you also need to remember that if your candidate is successful, (s)he is no longer **your** candidate. (S)he represents the whole constituency, and the **only** loyalty that (s)he owes is to the constituents that (s)he represents. That is part of what has gone wrong with the reputation of Parliament in the last 20 years. The task is for MPs to build integrity and trust with all of the voters in a way that comparatively few of our current MPs have managed to do in recent years.

Of course, the traditionalists in the main parties will protest that you do not need Independents. They will say that if you want to change a party it is better to do it from within. That may well be right, in theory – but all the evidence suggests that only loyal yes-men get selected as possible candidates, and then promoted to positions of influence. That could take a lifetime, and the voters of UK should not have to wait that long to get their democratic system rejuvenated.

How would you kickstart an idea like getting nominees for Independent candidates in an election?

Well you could begin by contacting the local media.

Plenty has been written about the abuses of the system, and there is a limit to how far the negative aspects of the story can be milked.

It's time to do something positive.

A telephone call to the editorial staff might be a good start to take the idea forward.

Can you do everything that ought to be done in the very

short period of time that is left? The honest answer is: "With great difficulty".

But you have to start somewhere, and the choice is between doing something in the next two months or so, or waiting for five years.

That is a no-brainer, isn't it?

Getting written commitments from all of the candidates in the constituency

Our representatives, and those who want to be our representatives, should have absolutely no doubts about the issues that concern us.

We should be bombarding all of our local parties with letters about our concerns, and making it clear that we require detailed answers before the Election.

Whilst many of these issues will, more properly, be dealt with by local councillors, it will nearly always be helpful to have the clout of Parliamentary candidates onside.

Early in 2008 I drafted the letter below (on the growing problem of knife-crime on the streets of UK). I sent it to all of the national newspapers. The hope was to stimulate an editor to investigate ways of getting MPs to do their jobs. As it happens, in 2008, a number of national newspapers began to wage vigorous campaigns on the issue: as a result knife-crime rose to the top of the national agenda and MPs became involved, irrespective of letters from constituents.

February 2008

Dear MP,

In 2007, fifty young people were murdered on the streets of UK. Many other people were injured as a result of knife crime. The figures for January 2008 do not seem to show much improvement. It is time that all political parties looked at ways of tackling the underlying problems.

Please tell me what your party intends to do:

(a) to punish those who commit crimes of violence,

(b) to deter those who may be on the fringes of such crimes, and

(c) to identify the factors that are likely to lead to such violence in the first place, and take steps to tackle them.

In the next two or three years you will be asking for my vote. In order to help me make an informed decision, please tell me what practical steps you intend to take to make our streets safer, and how you intend to work with members of other parties to make those steps a reality in the next twelve months.

Please acknowledge your receipt of this letter, and let me have a detailed reply within the next four weeks.

Yours sincerely

There is nothing special about the wording of this letter.

Plenty of people write passionate letters to their MPs.

We just need to send a lot more of them – especially in the next few weeks.

Our task, as voters, is to hold to account those who want to be our representatives. To do that we must be able to provide clear evidence that we have written, and that candidates for political office have responded in appropriate ways.

'Ordinary' people CAN make a difference, provided that we always remember that:

THE LOYALTIES OF AN MP ARE, IN ORDER OF PRIORITY, TO CONSTITUENTS, PARLIAMENT AND PARTY.

Whatever the issues that are dear to the hearts of voters, MPs will not know about them if we do not tell them.

Make sure that you tell them what the concern is.

Make sure that you ask them what the policy is.

Make sure that you ask your friends and family to do the same.

Make sure that the local media get a copy.

Make sure that the prospective candidates in your area are bombarded with letters on topics of concern – politicians judge the strength of public feeling on a matter by the size of their postbag.

Make sure that there can NEVER be an occasion in the future when an elected MP can say that (s)he did not realise that voters were so anxious about a particular issue.

Whatever the issue,

DO SOMETHING.

Determine a strategy for comparing the views of Parliamentary candidates

How do you choose which person to vote for?

Until the mid-nineties, most people voted for the party that they had always voted for.

That has changed. There is now a significant percentage (perhaps as much as 40% in recent elections) who do not make up their minds until late in the campaign – these are the Swing voters, and it is these people that are targeted by candidates.

If blogs are anything to go by then, there will be many more swing voters in the 2010 election.

How can our democratic processes help us to make an informed choice from the candidates available? We need to be able to evaluate the qualities of a real person, rather than blindly supporting the words that emanate from party headquarters. That may be bad news for local candidates, but it will be very good news for democracy in UK.

So, how do we get some sort of data for use in the comparison of Parliamentary candidates?

A few months ago, a frustrated voter came up with this idea on a blog:

> *"Before elections we ought to have a set of a dozen or so questions which all candidates should answer: the results could be tabulated and sent to all voters in the area."*

This sounds like a good idea, doesn't it? Perhaps it is already done in some constituencies: if it is, then it would be useful to learn about their experiences.

Here is a list of questions below to kick-off the idea.

Questions for Parliamentary candidates

a. *Have you been instructed by the relevant Parliamentary committee to reimburse the taxpayer for any expenses already paid to you? If so, how much has been demanded? Will you comply with that instruction?*

b. *What is the justification for the actions of so many MPs who have used their expenses system to fund a lavish lifestyle that is inaccessible to the majority of voters?*

c. *Do you accept that it is the voters who elect an MP as their representative and, therefore, it is to the voters, rather than a political party that an MP must give her/his first loyalty? How do you intend to demonstrate that loyalty to your constituents?*

d. *Do you agree with the findings of the Power Commission (2007) that the British political system will move into meltdown if nothing is done to re-engage MPs and voters? What do you intend to do in this constituency to re-engage people with the democratic political process?*

e. *In 1994, Lord Nolan stated that the seven Principles of Public Life are Honesty, Integrity, Openness, Objectivity, Leadership, Accountability, Selflessness. What evidence is there that you have these qualities?*

f. *Why do you think that so many voters regard many MPs as arrogant, greedy, and lacking in understanding of the needs of most voters?*

g. *What are you intending to do individually, and with your colleagues from all parties, in order to change that perception?*

h. *If elected, will you:*

   (a) *support in full the reforms on MPs expenses, proposed by the Kelly Committee?*

   (b) *vote for the principle, and support the practice, that every law in Britain applies equally to MPs as well as to all other citizens (eg pay freezes, pension rules, Freedom of Information, sex discrimination, smoking), and reject any proposal to raise the salary of MPs until any proposed national pay-freeze is lifted on all public-sector workers?*

   (c) *actively engage in consultation with your constituents, of all ages and political persuasions (face-to-face, in writing, by telephone) on matters of local and national concern?*

   (d) *support the setting-up of an appropriate consultative system that ensures that ideas can be generated amongst voters and used to inform and inspire national policies?*

(e) undertake to attend up to three formal meetings, every year, in different parts of the constituency, to which every voter is invited, and at which you will give an account of your stewardship in the previous year, and seek local opinions on issues that will arise in the future?

(f) work with local and national organisations, as well as with MPs of other political parties to reduce the level of violence on our streets and make them safer for everyone?

These ideas are not exclusive.

They clearly do not deal with issues that are specific to particular regions. They do not even deal with most national issues.

The important point to bear in mind is that all candidates in a particular area should address similar issues. They should be required to do so in no less than 100 words in any question.

The voters in a particular area might want to rewrite the document in part, or in its entirety. There is a real advantage in doing that, because then Party HQ will not be able to produce a party-line statement for all of their candidates to use.

What happens then?

It will only be useful if local media are willing to publish it.

Candidates who refuse to answer particular questions

will, in that refusal, be giving very eloquent answers on which voters will wish to make a judgement.

So, take the idea to the Editors of your local newspapers, or the Producer of relevant programmes on local radio and television. Will they run with it?

Assuming that the answer is "Yes", will they encourage voters to make suggestions for improving the questionnaire, and making it more relevant to local needs?

When the questionnaire has been agreed, send a copy to each candidate, and give her/him a deadline for answers.

Some candidates/parties will not take kindly to this strategy. In reality, it is a strategy for 'interviewing' candidates at a distance. Each one is being asked the same questions (this is important in any job interview because it complies with legislation relating to Equal Opportunities). The information is being published, so that all people who wish to vote can use the information, rather than rely on instinct and gut-reaction, to inform their vote (this is important because it complies with legislation on the Human Rights of the voter). The fact that an MP's answers will be made available to voters who need them in order to make a choice from the available candidates will comply with the Freedom of Information Act. Of course, some MPs have a problem with that Act: as is well known, some of them actually argued that details of their expense claims should be exempt from the FOI legislation.

Remember, the debate that we have to get started is not about the merits of one party compared to another, but about the worthiness of an individual to represent honest voters, to understand their hopes, to share their concerns and to make sure that those views are heard loudly and clearly in Westminster. Right now, it is not happening.

Voters are saying, more and more loudly, that they want MPs whose loyalties are to their constituents rather than their party. We should be prepared to tackle our Parliamentary candidates on this issue:

THE LOYALTIES OF AN MP ARE, IN ORDER OF PRIORITY, TO CONSTITUENTS, PARLIAMENT AND PARTY.

What are political parties for?

Well, certainly not to enable an MP to serve her/his constituents. Presumably, the original purpose of a political party was to get people with similar views elected so that, together, they had a chance of making significant changes in legislation and, perhaps, of making a significant improvement to the lives of people. There is a certain logic to acknowledging that if MPs cannot work together in a voting bloc then it is difficult to achieve anything.

That's a fair argument but, unfortunately, the realities of the party system leave much to be desired. Not only do we NOT need a party machine to get MPs to work for their constituents, we do not even need a party machine to get MPs to work together.

The evidence for that statement comes from the MPs themselves. In October 2009, following the publication of the Legg report, MPs of all parties, managed to get together and protest about the collective unfairness of it all: they even managed to formulate joint plans for legal action so that they could contest the demands that were being made of them. All of that was done within a matter of a couple of days.

MPs have demonstrated to all of us that they can work very effectively together in cross-party groups on matters that concern themselves. It would be good if they could demonstrate that skill when they are required to work on matters of direct concern to the voters!

It really is time that the mindsets of our MPs were changed.

A century or so ago, most MPs and members of political parties were not much involved in the lives of ordinary people. The perception is that it is still true in 2010.

A century or so ago, political parties and Parliament itself were little more than clubs to exclude the riff-raff or the toffs. Many voters think that that is still the case in 2010.

A century or so ago, MPs and members of political parties required deference from the voters and a respect for the belief that politicians knew what was best for everyone. Many of us doubt whether that has changed much today.

We are now in the 21st century, and things **ought** to have changed.

But sometimes it seems a bit like the late-nineteenth century world of Gilbert and Sullivan's operetta, 'Iolanthe'. Private Willis, on duty outside the House of

Commons, makes the observation:

> *"When, in that House, MPs divide,*
> *If they've a brain and cerebellum too,*
> *They've got to leave that brain outside,*
> *And vote just as their leaders tell 'em to."*

So, what's new? Just remember there are about 45 million voters in Britain.

There are 646 MPs. You could pack all of them in to a space about half the size of the goal area at Wembley. We CAN take them on – if we have the determination. But change will only happen if we are determined to make it happen.

These words are important. Only if we repeat them loud enough, and often enough, will our elected representatives get the message.

THE LOYALTIES OF AN MP ARE, IN ORDER OF PRIORITY, TO CONSTITUENTS, PARLIAMENT AND PARTY.

Chapter 4   ASKING AWKWARD QUESTIONS

This chapter is about what we must do when we know the date of the General Election

There are three key, and frequently repeated, ideas in this chapter:

(a) Most voters in UK are angered by the usual strategy of "Yah-Boo' politics.

(b) The expenses scandal has undermined the democratic process in UK, because now voters distrust MPs even more than they did before.

(c) All voters have a duty to ensure that our elected representatives cannot easily ignore us again.

The date of the next General Election is at the discretion of the Prime Minister. He will, of course, choose a date when things are proceeding well, or possibly, are less negative than normal. This is likely to be easier said than done!

What should we be trying to do during the Election campaign?

The key role is to establish the idea that

ALL VOTERS HAVE A DUTY TO ENSURE THAT OUR ELECTED REPRESENTATIVES CANNOT EASILY IGNORE US AGAIN

In the General Election 2010, we, the voters, may need some underlying principles to guide us, as well as focus the minds of Parliamentary candidates. Such basic principles need to be discussed and personalised by groups of individuals: they certainly should not be taken as a job-lot. The main themes from this book might act as a starting point for defining the way to tackle prospective Parliamentary candidates.

A. 'Ordinary' people can make a difference.
B. Each of us must vote.
C. People around the world are dying in the fight for democracy: in the UK democracy is allowed to die, because people cannot be bothered to fight for it.
D. Democracy is too important to leave in the hands of politicians.
E. The expenses scandal has undermined the democratic process in UK, because now voters distrust MPs even more than they did before.
F. A healthy democracy encourages active participation of all of the people.
G. The loyalties of a Member of Parliament are, in order of priority, to:
   (i)   constituents,
   (ii)   Parliament,
   (iii)   political party.
H. MPs have a duty to consult regularly with their constituents, of all political persuasions.
I. All voters have a duty to ensure that our elected representatives cannot easily ignore us again.
J. MPs work for voters and, therefore, voters must have significant representation in discussions of the roles and remuneration of MPs.

K. One of the roles of the new generation of MPs is to clean-up Parliament.
L. Most voters in UK are angered by the usual strategy of "Yah-Boo" politics.
M. The expenses scandal is not a party-political issue: the abuse has involved members of all parties.

We could call this, or any other, list of strategies "In It Together".

The title 'In It Together' ought to go down well with many politicians. It was a political slogan in speeches at one party conference. It also has the merit of being a phrase that no prospective MP could possibly disagree with in public. We know, of course that, in private, many MPs **will** disagree with the idea that they should be 'In It Together' with the rest of the people in UK. The expenses scandal makes it quite clear that some MPs believe that whilst ordinary people, like you and me, are 'In It Together' (with all of our family, friends and neighbours), they (the professional politicians) are something rather more upmarket, and deserve special, and exclusive, treatment. They have set themselves apart, and have no wish to be 'In It Together' with the likes of you and me.

That approach needs to be challenged.

But, the title is unimportant – it is what we are prepared do that is important.

We all know that election campaigns are about spin rather than substance.

They involve:

- **a manifesto produced by a group of like-minded mates;**

- **stage-managed walkabouts amongst the voters by candidates;**

- **stage-managed 'talkabouts' by candidates, many of whom rarely communicate with most of the constituents once they get elected;**

- **evasion of awkward questions by giving answers to questions that were not asked;**

- **visits to institutions, the choice of which depends whether candidates are defending their own achievements, or debasing those of their opponents;**

- **criticisms of the policies of other parties, instead of explanations of their own;**

- **character assassination of opponents;**

- **photo-opportunities and soundbites;**

- **hypocrisy.**

As indicated in chapter 2, the proportion of people in UK who no longer vote in General Elections has steadily increased to a massive 40%. Our politicians have come up with a number of solutions to this problem: it is difficult to think of any of those solutions that have been successful. This is possibly because politicians have not actually listened to those who have abdicated from democracy. Instead, they have listened to party members who have come up with a political point-scoring strategy, masquerading as a 'good idea' – irrespective of whether it is grounded in reality. The result is a frequent identification of the wrong reasons for the increasing number of disillusioned, disenfranchised and disengaged people in UK.

It is hardly surprising that politicians have not considered blaming themselves. The fact that they all continue campaign antics such as those listed above, seems designed to cause an active disengagement of people from the political process.

Every time that we have a General Election, we tell political parties that:

MOST VOTERS IN UK ARE ANGERED BY THE USUAL STRATEGY OF 'YAH-BOO' POLITICS

And every time, most politicians do absolutely nothing to alter their in-grained behaviour. In other words, they listen to voters' comments on their behaviour as carefully as they listen to the rest of our comments – ie not at all unless, of course, our comments support their own partisan views.

Our election process involves candidates doing what they always have done. As a result fewer people want to be involved in the process. When our politicians spend time – a lot of time - in some of the most desolate and deprived areas of UK and see and hear the desperate results of decades of neglect, only then will they begin to understand some of the harsh realities of life.

It might be useful to press your candidates on how often they have visited difficult parts of the constituency, what they have identified as the underlying problems, and how they intend to tackle them.

Setting the agenda for the General Election in your constituency

The way in which we do democratic elections in UK involves the politician doing the talking, and the voters doing the listening. That needs to change.

When the campaign is launched, the candidates will be out in force, with the local party members in attendance – it is just as well that there are plenty of reasonably well-known local party members around, because most voters will not have seen their current MP since 2005 when (s)he last wandered the streets seeking votes.

If your constituency is a marginal (and a lot of them are likely to be marginals this time round), it is likely that someone senior in the party will also visit to smile and shake hands.

If your constituency has a newly-selected candidate (and there will be a lot of those), then it is also likely that a senior member of the party will come along to support her/him.

The agenda is all fairly artificial – the spontaneity is stage-managed, and the agenda is determined by the Party. That means that the candidate and her/his foot-soldiers are required to sell particular issues in the Party Manifesto, and make much of the faults of their opponents. We, the voters, are going to be told what the Party/candidate wants us to hear. That is not necessarily what we need to know in order to make an informed vote.

Voters may be invited ask questions, but the usual practice is to give the same answers, whatever the questions: we have all seen that happen on television. There may well be party members in the crowd who are planted to ask questions which the candidate can then 'answer' to the exclusion of less-palatable questions from other members of the crowd. If a number of people ask questions simultaneously, candidates will, of course, choose not to hear the ones that could be difficult.

In the past, the whole charade has been a one-sided dialogue between the bemused (voter) and the complacent (politician), or between the involuntarily mute (voter) and the selectively deaf (politician). That is what politicians do. That is how they fight elections. In anyone's language that spells contempt.

That is what will happen in 2010 if we give them half a chance.

If we are to start making a difference to the effectiveness of our democratic processes at this election, then we must give candidates a hard time when they come pleading for our votes. We need to be much more proactive – we have to go out and ask awkward questions. Do NOT let politicians set the Agenda. Stand up - Speak Up - Be Counted.

This time they will have to earn every letter of that word H-O-N-O-U-R-A-B-L-E that they are seeking to put before their names.

Let's start with a personal agenda – A Voter's Agenda.

That will be a novel experience for voters and for the candidates, since it will not have occurred to most politicians that voters could have what is, in effect, a tick-list of requirements.

What might be included on that tick-list of questions? Well, of course, they are up to the individual voter. Here are some general ones that may be relevant to some of us:

1. WHAT SORT OF PERSON DO I WANT TO REPRESENT ME IN PARLIAMENT?

This question is a vital one. It is an obvious one, arising from the fact that:

THE EXPENSES SCANDAL HAS UNDERMINED THE DEMOCRATIC PROCESS IN UK, BECAUSE NOW VOTERS DISTRUST MPs EVEN MORE THAN THEY DID BEFORE

That question has absolutely nothing to do with the Party that a candidate represents, and a great deal to do with the integrity, transparency and straightforwardness of the candidate. It also involves a number of politically-incorrect issues, such as:

- **family experiences (does the candidate have children)?**
- **gender,**
- **ethnic background,**
- **education,**
- **career background and progression, and**
- **sexual orientation.**

It is politically incorrect to ask about such things, in case the question causes offence, and leads a voter not to vote for a candidate.

It is politically stupid to ignore such issues if they enable a voter to choose a representative who has the same sort of life-experiences as her/himself. We do, after all, live in a representative democracy. Presumably this means that our democratically elected representatives must be, well…representative.

If a candidate has experienced the sort of realities of life that you are facing, you may feel that (s)he understands the real issues that you must live with.

If a candidate lives in a similar area to you, you may feel that (s)he is likely to understand the problems that you have to face – whatever they may be.

If a candidate uses the same sorts of public services that you do – NHS hospitals, state schools, public transport – you may feel that this person is more likely to generate improvements than might be the case if the candidate uses private services.

If a candidate has worked in the public sector or the private sector, you will be able to make a judgement as to the way in which your own experiences tie in with those of the candidate.

2. DO I WANT TO KNOW WHAT IS WRONG WITH A CANDIDATE'S POLITICAL OPPONENTS?

Perhaps you do – in which case the aggressive and combative candidate may well be your style of representative. The fact is that:

MOST VOTERS IN UK ARE ANGERED BY THE STRATEGY OF "YAH-BOO" POLITICS

If that includes you, then candidates need to be interrupted loudly and clearly once they start the usual tactic of slagging-off opponents. You and the rest of the voters are there to hear of the merits of the party represented by this candidate, not the faults of the opponents. Does any democracy need a candidate who thinks that (s)he is the source of enlightenment to voters who are too thick to work out the faults of political parties? We are perfectly capable of making up our own minds about opponents and their policies. If we need additional advice, we certainly will not seek it from another politician.

The normal character-assassination that is incorporated into campaigning suggests a level of arrogance that has beset the House of Commons for far too long. Such candidates are surplus to requirements, and should go and get a job in the real world.

3. DO I HAVE A CONCERN ABOUT THE HONESTY OF MPs?

THE EXPENSES SCANDAL HAS UNDERMINED THE DEMOCRATIC PROCESS IN UK, BECAUSE NOW VOTERS DISTRUST MPs EVEN MORE THAN THEY DID BEFORE

This is an important matter, because it says something about the attitude of profligate MPs towards the taxpayers of UK.

For an MP who has made inappropriate expense claims

The obvious point to make is that MPs who have abused the system should be publicly reminded of that, and their moral duty to reimburse the taxpayer. For instance, (s)he could be asked questions such as:

"How can you justify those claims?"

"Are you required to pay anything back?"

"How much?"

"Will you comply?"

"Is it right for MPs to claim £100 a week for food, when that is in excess of the total pension, agreed by Parliament, for people of 65 years or more?"

"MPs would have to eat even if they weren't MPs, so why do they need taxpayers to pay an additional allowance for their food?"

"Do you know how much (item from supermarket) costs?"

Somewhere in the answers, there is likely to be something along the lines of "It's all within the rules".

The question from you could be "Who made the rules?" or "Don't you think that it is hypocritical for MPs to tell the voters that you understand their difficulties, when your expense claims seem to suggest the exact opposite?"

For those MPs who have behaved less than honourably, it may be that the words that they are saying now are rather different to their behaviour of a year or so ago. It may be worth asking what has made them change their mind – is it because of instructions from senior officials, fear of losing votes, or a conversion to the view that MPs are accountable to taxpayers?

There is some homework to do if we are to challenge our sitting MP.

Make sure that you go through the data that is already available online.

You could start with the Daily Telegraph website, where you will find a breakdown of the expenses that have been incurred.

You could get the summary of MPs' expenses given in the Daily Telegraph supplement of 20 June 2009 (The Complete Expenses file).

<u>For an MP who has used the expenses system appropriately</u>

Whilst that should be noted publicly, those individuals need to be challenged about their perceptions of what goes on around them. Every MP knew the nature of the expenses system. It is highly likely that most MPs knew that some of their colleagues were abusing the system. We might ask such MPs:

"Why did you not challenge those who were less-than-honest?"

"Why did you not use your influence to expose a manifestly corrupt system?"

"If you lack the courage to tackle abuses in Westminster, how can we be sure that you would have the courage to tackle some of the life-threatening abuses on the streets of UK?"

"Can you understand that policies to encourage 'ordinary' people to expose Benefit Cheats sound very hollow, when MPs will not expose expenses cheats?"

<u>For those candidates who have never served before in Westminster</u>

We need to ensure that they have learned the lessons from the expenses scandal. A question such as this might be useful:

"Do you accept that a large number of MPs have behaved dishonestly, with no consideration of the hardships suffered by taxpayers?"

4. WILL THIS CANDIDATE BE STRONG ENOUGH TO WORK WITH OTHERS TO CLEAN UP PARLIAMENT

In the new Parliament, perhaps half of the MPs will be new. Of course, that means that the other half will still be the old school, some of whom will be only too willing to initiate the new ones into the rituals of the past.

But change will only happen if there are people in Parliament who will not be whipped into some party line, or some archaic system that justifies its practices by saying that this is the way we have always done things round here.

We need to find out what evidence there is that a candidate has stood up against wrongdoers, and is willing to make her/himself unpopular in doing so.

We need to be sure that a candidate is strong enough to state that members of her/his own party have behaved disgracefully, and no longer deserve the title of Honourable Member.

Any weakness in a response to that question might suggest that this candidate does not have the spine for the task of cleaning-up Parliament.

Once again, the vital issue at stake is this:

THE EXPENSES SCANDAL HAS UNDERMINED THE DEMOCRATIC PROCESS IN UK, BECAUSE NOW VOTERS DISTRUST MPs EVEN MORE THAN THEY DID BEFORE

The task of the new generation of MPs is to clean-up Parliament.

That is no role for the faint-hearted.

5. WHAT POLICY DOES YOUR PARTY HAVE ON......?

The candidates will want to tell you about all of the promises that their party is making in the new manifesto.

Make sure that (s)he keeps to the point, and answers the question that you asked.

It is useful to have copies of previous manifesto commitments: the Labour, Conservative and Liberal Democrat manifestoes for the last three General Elections are all available online.

Ask for comments about promises in those manifestoes that were not fulfilled when the party was in Government or in charge of a Council.

Ask how we can have confidence in the trustworthiness

of a party that makes a promise and then does not fulfil it when in a position to do so.

The result of the grilling that we give to candidates should leave them under no illusions that voters believe that this election is about making our democracy a great deal healthier. It has become unhealthy because:

THE EXPENSES SCANDAL HAS UNDERMINED THE DEMOCRATIC PROCESS IN UK, BECAUSE NOW VOTERS DISTRUST MPs EVEN MORE THAN THEY DID BEFORE

Chapter 5 TAKING ON THE NEW PARLIAMENT

There are five key ideas in this chapter:

(a) **Every voter has a duty to ensure that our elected representatives cannot easily ignore us again**

(b) **The role of the new generation of MPs is to clean-up Parliament;**

(c) **The loyalties of an MP are, in order of priority, to constituents, Parliament and political party**

(d) **MPs work for the voter and, therefore, voters must have significant representation in discussions of the roles and remuneration of MPs**

(e) **A healthy democracy encourages the participation of all of the people.**

By May or June 2010, a new Government will be in place.

If one party achieves an overall majority in the General Election, then it probably does not much matter which of the parties it is. That sweeping statement is based on the ideas that:

(a) Each of the parties has a reputation for not listening to the people;

(b) Many voters believe that there is little to choose between the parties;

(c) Some MPs of all parties have been guilty of appalling abuses of the expenses system;

(d) Many MPs in the main parties have long-standing reputations of dismissive, arrogant and contemptuous attitudes towards voters – especially those voters who supported other parties;

(e) In Parliament, many MPs in the main parties behave like rival gangs of kids in school playgrounds.

Clearly, this is not good enough.

So, what is our longer-term strategy for sorting things out?

Of course, that depends whether we had the will-power to do anything useful **before or during** the General Election campaign.

The unequivocal message that we should be giving is this:

ALL VOTERS HAVE A DUTY TO ENSURE THAT OUR ELECTED REPRESENTATIVES CANNOT EASILY IGNORE US AGAIN

If voters have made their message clear, then all MPs will recognise that they need to demonstrate their re-engagement with voters.

If voters have done their job well, all MPs will have a clear understanding that we will be watching them carefully.

If voters have done their job well, then we will have documentary evidence of commitments to the idea that consultation with constituents is a part of the task of every MP.

But, whatever the good intentions of voters in the next few weeks, we will only make a difference to our democracy if we hold MPs to their promises.

So what do we need to do to regain and retain control of our MPs, and ensure that we, the voters, are a real part of the democratic country of UK? Let's just remind ourselves of the important principle, frequently mentioned in early chapters – democracy is too important to leave in the hands of politicians – indeed we could make it even more damning **– politics is too important to leave in the hands of politicians!**

Here are some suggestions. They are no more than that. For too long our democracy has been built on the idea that a group of representatives in Westminster (who are about as unrepresentative of real people as it is possible to get) know best. They propose ideas, implement them, and then decide that those ideas have been a success (using criteria that were invented once the outcomes were known). The perceptions of everyone else may be different, but politics in Britain (and probably in most other places as well) works on the principle that if an MP says something often enough then people will believe her/him: in many cases, even the MP begins to believe her/his own hype!

So, the ideas here are merely suggestions to stimulate discussion amongst voters. Whether the system in UK needs some, all or none of these, is up to people to decide. Those people are the voters who have, hitherto, been excluded from virtually every discussion that affects their lives.

Each of these ideas is about involving the electorate more in democracy – after all, Lincoln told us that democracy is of, **by** and for the people. Unless anyone is taking the serious position that Abraham Lincoln was wrong, then it's time to ask whether more of us should become more actively involved, or take steps to ensure that our views are heard. Greater involvement might well be a way to reduce the cynicism and disengagement of people, and achieve a higher turnout at elections.

1. A CONTRACT BETWEEN MPs AND CONSTITUENTS

Assuming that your MP responded to a questionnaire similar to the one given on page 00, you have what is in effect, a Contract between the MP and those who voted for her/him. After all, it was on the basis of the answers that this candidate gave to the questions that a majority of voters in the constituency chose this person, rather than the other candidates. The contract should be binding, and the MP should expect to be called to account if there is evidence that (s)he has not fulfilled her/his part of the agreement. That is the way that employment contracts work in the real world, and so it should be for MPs. In this case, voters have delivered their side of the arrangement – the vote. Now it is up to the MP to fulfil her/his part of the bargain.

It is important to continue to emphasise the point, frequently repeated in this book:

THE LOYALTIES OF AN MP ARE, IN ORDER OF PRIORITY, TO CONSTITUENTS, PARLIAMENT AND PARTY.

2. CLEANING-UP WESTMINSTER

On that same theme of an MP's duty to the constituents, we should be looking at ways of enshrining this idea into politics and the party-system as a whole.

ONE OF THE MOST IMPORTANT ROLES OF MPS IN THE NEW PARLIAMENT IS TO CLEAN-UP WESTMINSTER

In the new Parliament there will be a great deal said about changing the culture of Westminster. If the culture really is changed, it ought to be to something that is substantially better than the present. Of course, a great deal depends on what is agreed. In the new Parliament there will be many MPs who are new: that is good, because they will not be steeped in the irrelevant and arcane rituals of the Gentleman's club that is Parliament.

But, it is not new MPs who will be making the decisions about the new culture. Most of that is being done now, before the election. It is being done on behalf of the voters, but not BY the voters.

It is amazing that the restructuring of Parliamentary procedures and the activities of our representatives is being carried out by a group consisting of MPs, civil servants and hand-picked outsiders – to the exclusion of those who are represented.

When will that exclusive group ask voters for their views about the changes that are necessary? I think that the answer will be along the lines of "In your dreams, mate."

It is still not clear whether MPs will vote on the acceptability of the resulting proposals (acceptable, that is, to MPs).

What is totally clear is that ordinary voters will have no chance of making their views known on the new proposals.

It is amazing that, at a time when there is acknowledgement that there must be a total shake-up in the culture of greed and privilege in Parliament, the largest stakeholder in the system – the taxpayer – has not even been invited to take part in the discussions or asked for her/his views. This is yet another application of the principle that 'Daddy and mummy know best'. That archaic principle has no place in a democracy. It is no way to treat voters. But it is happening – right now.

Can you imagine any commercial organisation in which negotiations on Conditions of Service took place between workers and some external body, with no input from the employers? Of course it would not be allowed to happen – except in Parliament.

MPs WORK FOR THE VOTERS AND, THEREFORE, VOTERS MUST HAVE SIGNIFICANT REPRESENTATION IN DISCUSSIONS OF THE ROLES AND REMUNERATION OF MPs.

3. GETTING PEOPLE INVOLVED IN CHANGE

When Mr Brown took over as Prime Minister in June 2007, one interesting proposal that he made was that we need 'Citizens' Juries' to generate ideas and feed them back to Government. The idea was roundly ridiculed by politicians of all parties, civil servants and the media. It disappeared without trace.

That was a pity. There are plenty of ideas out here. Good ideas do not reside solely in the minds of politicians and civil servants. Indeed, the evidence of the last thirty years might suggest that there are very few good ideas that have been generated by **any** politicians, irrespective of party.

'Ordinary' people may not walk in the Corridors of Power, or be academics or executives, or rich, but the ideas are here, and they are, as usual, ignored. The policy of 'No riff-raff' seems alive and well when it comes to ideas from 'ordinary' people for improving the lives of people in this country. That is part of what is wrong with our democracy – the professional experts chat and pontificate and decide and implement: the rest of us don't even get a look-in.

A HEALTHY DEMOCRACY ENCOURAGES THE PARTICIPATION OF ALL OF THE PEOPLE

What is the solution? Is it possible for a group of 'ordinary' people to analyse particular issues, and propose original solutions? Of course it is. All that is needed is the political will to recognise that there is an immense amount of wisdom and expertise on the streets of UK, and it needs to be tapped if we are to improve the quality of life in this country. A Citizens' Forum is exactly the right way to generate new ideas – that is probably why the Prime Minister's idea was so roundly condemned.

In any case, whatever the outcome of such a 'Citizens' Forum', it really cannot be any worse than a forum of MPs, generating reams of paper, and achieving nothing.

So, how about groups of voters, set up around the country, tackling three main topics:

(a) re-engaging people with democracy;

(b) making our streets safer;

(c) defining the duties, and conditions of service for MPs.

Each of these issues needs to be tackled. Each of them needs fresh ideas. Those new ideas will, in part, be solved by people at the sharp end of the problem, rather than by a committee, some of whose members seem to have been selected because of their remoteness from real life. Tackling even one of these three issues effectively in the next five years will do much to regenerate trust between the people and their representatives.

4. SELECTION OF CANDIDATES TO REPRESENT THE PEOPLE

The manifestoes of our local candidates provide a wide range of diverse personal information, such as biography, achievements and interests, but there is rarely anything there that enables us to make useful comparisons. This omission is relatively easy to remedy using an approach that is well-established in UK. It should, therefore, be popular with all of the political parties.

As consumers, many of us make important buying decisions by comparing what is available. Look at the websites of major retailers of electrical goods – such as washing machines. The largest retailers will provide comparative information to enable purchasers to make a rational choice.

We should be grateful to politicians of the two largest parties who, when in government, made it mandatory that consumers were supplied with information to help them choose. This applied not only to items such as washing machines, but also to organisations as diverse as councils, hospitals and schools. Using such information, together with relevant statistical data (e.g. mortality rates, examination/test results) consumers are, allegedly, in a much better position that they once were, to make rational choices. The two largest parties are totally committed to the idea of rational choice, based on facts. They are also committed to the idea of League Tables designed to highlight high and low performers.

Why do we not do something similar with our Parliamentary candidates in the future? For instance:

(a) We could use the expenses data to work out whether our present MP has been expensive to maintain, and also assess whether (s)he has given good value for money. This could be linked to a system of performance-related pay.

(b) We could publish details of her/his attendance in the House of Commons, and the regularity of attendance in constituency surgeries.

(c) We might evaluate the relevance to the constituency of an MP's 'fact-finding' visits overseas, as well as the cost to the taxpayer.

(d) We could work on criteria for assessing her/his record of achievement for constituents.

Of course, that does not help us to assess the likely effectiveness of those who are standing as Parliamentary candidates for the first time. In order to do that effectively we have to rely upon their answers to our questionnaire. This is similar to the way in which the rest of us have to rely upon the statements that candidates give at interviews for jobs, or the statements that manufacturers make about the merits of their products. If, of course, those statements prove to be less than honest, then employers or purchasers have recourse to the law. Much the same could apply to newly-elected MPs.

Of course, figures give an illusion of accuracy but, like most government figures, and the league tables that they generate, mere figures do not even begin to evaluate the quality of the contribution that an MP makes to the democracy of Britain. However, it would be a useful issue to consider in the lifetime of the new Parliament. It would ensure that MPs would be held to the same reasonable criteria of effectiveness in their employment as the rest of us in the real world.

5. TACKLING DISILLUSIONMENT

In 2008, Tom Harris, a Labour MP, published some comments on his website. They caused a national debate. The theme was "Why are we so miserable?".

It really ought not to have been necessary for him to ask – but he did.

In Appendix 2, I include the comments that I sent in response.

It is unfortunate that an MP such as Mr Harris had to ask the question, but his ignorance of the answer may well indicate that there are plenty of other MPs who have much the same question on their minds. Perhaps some of them have lost touch with reality. Who knows?

The important issue is that we should not allow it to happen again.

MPs really are expected to be 'In It Together" with the rest of us.

We need to tell them what the problems are.

We need structures that will ensure that MPs are engaged regularly with the lives and the needs of their constituents.

When they understand the abject misery in which so many people have to live, then they may begin to do things that will make a difference.

That is what the job of an MP is all about.

We need a Forum that will ensure that our local MPs are regularly informed about the harsh realities of life of all of their constituents. That may be at a series of open meetings in their constituencies, or it may involve temporary residence in difficult areas of the constituency – for instance in the Parliamentary recesses when they cannot be involved in the rigours of legislation.

How it is done is a matter for debate between employee (MP) and employer (voter). The fact that such a role is necessary is unarguable.

It might go some way to ensuring that MPs do not ask stupid questions like "Why are we so miserable?

6. LAYING THE GROUNDWORK FOR A LONG-TERM COMMITMENT TO CHANGE

A very large number of the current, and previous, generations of MPs have demonstrated a total lack of understanding of their relationships with the voters, as well as the need for towering, and demonstrable, personal integrity.

After the General Election of 2010, it is possible that voters might heed the pleas of MPs that we move on from the expenses calamity of 2009. That might be a reasonable proposal, provided that it is backed up with something like an agreement on the aims of our democracy in this country. During the period of office of the next Government, we should be presenting all political parties with a requirement that they formulate a contract with the electorate.

One of the more inspiring ideas to come from US is the Republican Party's 'Contract with America'. It was launched in 1994, and is included as Appendix 3.

The detailed legislative content of that contract may well be only marginally relevant to UK, but the principles on which the Contract is based are far more appropriate. The Contract with UK needs to propose ideas such as these:

(a) There will be a requirement that all laws that apply to the rest of the country apply equally to Parliament;

(b) A major, independent auditing firm will be selected to conduct a comprehensive audit of Parliament and Government for waste, fraud or abuse;

(c) There will be a reduction in the number of MPs by one-third;

(d) Think-tanks composed of ordinary voters will be set up, in order to generate ideas on defined areas of activity, and inform political policies;

(e) All MPs will have clearly-defined lines of accountability to constituents;

(f) Active consideration will be given to re-engaging people in democracy.

The Contract with America seems to have got lost in a welter of hypocrisy, double-dealing and apathy – sadly much of it from the party that wrote the document in the first place. That will of course, provide all of the ammunition needed by MPs in this country to argue against producing a Contract with UK. "It won't work here" will be the knee-jerk response from many politicians. Unfortunately, the knee-jerk response from many voters is that our democratic system is not working well in UK anyway.

We need something as fundamental as a Contract between representatives and people. The principles and the promises need to be open to discussion across the country – sadly, in the present climate of distrust and mutual contempt there is little chance of producing the cultural change needed by tinkering with details. And that's what we seem to be committed to in UK – well, at least those in Westminster seem to be committed to it.

Unfortunately, messing about with odd details, agreed in

some committee Room in the House of Commons, by a group of people, none of whom represent real people, will not inspire trust with the voters.

It would be rather better to consider what went wrong in US, and develop our own Contract to overcome those difficulties.

Finally, read the last words of that Contract with America:

Respecting the judgment of our fellow citizens as we seek their mandate for reform, we hereby pledge our names to this Contract with America.

Are these words just fanciful twaddle?

Perhaps.

They could be merely a new version of politician-speak, meaning ' Vote for Me', in which case, they will be of considerable interest to our own politicians.

Whatever America may have done with its Contract with America is largely immaterial to UK. They may have thrown it out, or shelved it, or ridiculed it. We can learn from their mistakes.

More importantly, we can make it work, if we have the strength of purpose, the vision and the determination.

If we are to change our political system for the better in the long-term, we must never lose sight of principles like these. Just as importantly, our representatives must never be allowed to lose sight of them. If they show any signs of doing so, then they need to be reminded – loudly, and clearly:

A HEALTHY DEMOCRACY ENCOURAGES THE PARTICIPATION OF ALL OF THE PEOPLE

MPs WORK FOR THE VOTERS AND, THEREFORE, VOTERS MUST HAVE SIGNIFICANT REPRESENTATION IN DISCUSSIONS OF THE ROLE OF AN MP.

THE LOYALTIES OF AN MP ARE, IN ORDER OF PRIORITY, TO CONSTITUENTS, PARLIAMENT AND PARTY.

ONE OF THE MOST IMPORTANT ROLES OF MPS IN THE NEW PARLIAMENT IS TO CLEAN-UP WESTMINSTER

EVERY VOTER HAS A DUTY TO ENSURE THAT OUR ELECTED REPRESENTATIVES CANNOT EASILY IGNORE THEIR US AGAIN

Chapter 6   REGAINING A DEMOCRACY WORTH FIGHTING FOR

PEOPLE AROUND THE WORLD ARE DYING IN THE FIGHT FOR DEMOCRACY: IN THE UK DEMOCRACY IS ALLOWED TO DIE BECAUSE PEOPLE CANNOT BE BOTHERED TO FIGHT FOR IT

As was stated in Chapter 1, this book was written out of sheer anger and frustration.

We have known for YEARS that our Parliamentary system in UK is founded upon a lie.

That lie is that we can trust our representatives to represent us with integrity, and with loyalty.

It's a dreadful statement to make, but it's true.

The fury felt by the public regarding the expenses of MPs is merely the tip of a great iceberg of anger that so many of us have felt for decades, about their behaviour and perceived attitude towards us, the voters. So many of us believe that they are arrogant, dismissive, patronising, unsympathetic, and just plain uninterested in the hopes and fears of the voters.

Until 2009 those 'beliefs' were just that. There was no rigorous evidence – just a lot of perception based on body language and off-the-cuff comments.

All that has changed with the publication of the Expenses data. Now we have hard evidence that our worst fears are actually real. We have been ripped-off by those who should be the guardians of integrity and democracy in UK.

It has to change.

There have seen some voices of moderation.

The Archbishop of Canterbury has suggested that we lay off MPs because they now have the message.

Some MPs have said that it is time to move on now, because the point has been made by the voters.

Another MP tried the emotional blackmail strategy, and suggested that if the public kept banging-on about the expenses scandal then there would be suicides amongst some MPs.

Those pleas are all very well, but the fact remains that our politicians have betrayed our trust for years.

They have known that we know about it for years.

They have done nothing to regain that trust.

Now they are paying the price for that complacency.

We must ensure that we do not tackle their complacency with our complacency.

This year, we have the chance to make a real improvement to the way in which we do democracy in Britain. Before, during and after the Election we, the voters, can make a difference, because we have the hard evidence that very many MPs are not to be trusted with taxpayers' money, at least they can't be trusted with it when it comes to funding their lavish lifestyle.

In cases whether that has happened, the voters need to make it clear that the MPs are surplus to requirements. They are not needed. We can do without them. Their wishes are irrelevant. They are expendable (from the point of view of the well-being of British democracy).

What we should be left with is a group of MPs who are worthy of our trust, who represent out interests with integrity, who listen and respond to our views with respect, and who stimulate the citizens of UK to take part in the democratic process.

Such MPs will be well worth an enhanced salary.

They will also be well worth the title 'Honourable Member'.

The responsibility of voters is to ensure that our children get a democracy worth having, and in which they want to participate.

The next generation deserve a better representative democracy than the one that we have at the moment in UK – at least they deserve better representatives.

When we do that we will have changed from 'Ordinary' people who can make a difference, to 'Extraordinary' people who have made a difference.

Let's do something about changing it.

Appendix 1

21 May 2009

Dear Editor,

BROKEN BRITAIN

Was your petition for a General Election written by a politician?

It offers two alternatives – agree with it, or shut up.

You do not appear to want to know how many there are in the latter category.

With respect, I suggest that you are demonstrating exactly what is wrong with our MPs: they do not take the views of dissenters seriously, either. I don't remember a time when they ever did. Do you?

That is the problem.

The politicians tell us that they are sorry that the voters lost trust in their MPs two weeks ago.

You know that they are talking rubbish.

After all, for years, you have reported that MPs have about as much moral clout as a piece of soggy tissue-paper, and a similar amount of respect amongst the voters.

The truth is that the present debacle is merely the latest in the pathetic saga about moral wimps who seriously believe themselves to be above the law.

Believe it or not, MPs have not yet got the message that things need to change. Many do still believe that there is nothing fundamentally wrong with the current system of expenses, and the practice of being patronising to voters, and playing their petulant party political games.

We have a government with too many members who have a flexible approach to the value of integrity. We have a government-in-waiting with a similar lot of moral misfits.

It is not my idea of a vibrant democracy to replace one lot with the other. Surely you do not want that either.

Calling an election in a few weeks will ensure that this is precisely what WILL happen.

Reform of our system will come from the people. We need a few months to do effective ground work – if we do not have time for that then voters will have to choose between the same set of unsatisfactory alternatives as usual.

That must not happen.

I would like to see a large body of Independent MPs that will push forward some root-and-branch reforms to move our system of democracy into the 21st century. Action must be taken to ensure that never again can British democracy be abused in the way that we have seen in recent years.

I hope that your newspaper will do its part to encourage men and women across the country to put themselves forward as MPs, independent of any of the political parties, dedicated to the reform of our democracy.

I hope that you will support them by giving intensive coverage in the run-up to an election to ensure that the message of democratic reform in UK gets across.

We need a party that can be supported by disillusioned voters. A party that stands for integrity, democracy and renewal…….. I really do hope that you will be supporting rational and organised reform of yet one more aspect of Broken Britain.

Appendix 2
WELL, WHY <u>ARE</u> WE SO MISERABLE?

Tom Harris, MP asks "Why are we all so miserable?"

Let me explain, Mr Harris.

First off, Mr Harris, why did you need to ask? Read the blogs from real people over the last few years – they are full of cynicism and bitterness. Over the last thirty years, young people have become more and more disenchanted with Britain: far too many do not see a future worth having. We have been pretty miserable for a long time, but few in power were (or are) interested. No wonder we are still so miserable.

Of course, the immediate problem is an economic one: that is enough to make anyone miserable. But there are far more deep-seated problems. Too many people in Britain see our society as unfair, shallow, hypocritical, mechanistic and greedy. No wonder we are so miserable!

Far too many people who love Britain and who work hard see less and less point in doing so. Many honestly believe that working hard is a mug's game because the skyvers are rewarded, and the workers foot the bill. No wonder we are so miserable!

Many people believe that the law is more interested in dealing with the soft and easy targets than with big crime. A majority of law-abiding people in Britain regard the national system of law-enforcement as a joke. No wonder we are so miserable!

The slagging-off that goes on in the name of party politics has now been raised to an art-form, and is described as 'reality TV'. Is that really what real life is all about? Is that why TV is celebrating it? Is that what we should be aiming for? No wonder we are so miserable!

We are fed the details of the glamorous lives of 'celebrities' on TV and in the press. Should we be trying to mimic their lifestyles? The trouble is that if we do, many of us discover, too late, that our bank accounts don't match. No wonder we are so miserable!

If any of us want to do some serious thinking about issues of right and wrong, we are largely on our own – Coronation Street or Eastenders might possibly help, but sadly, religion, politics and the law no longer connect with real people. No wonder we are so miserable!

If we want to feel safe on the streets of Britain, tough. It ain't going to happen. Far too many people, young and old, do not feel safe. In 2008, there are actually no-go areas in Britain, just as there were a couple of centuries ago. No wonder we are so miserable!

In 2008, young people and not-so-young people want to know what the rules are. The bad news is that there aren't any rules that reflect what we believe about the way we do things in Britain. In Britain we seem to have abandoned them, in case they upset someone. Sadly, the absence of any obvious underlying rules ends up by upsetting everyone. No wonder we are so miserable!

Mr Harris's question deserves serious thought. The initial response was cheap party political jibes. That sort of knee-jerk political claptrap from MPs is part of the problem. It is their time-honoured way of ensuring that difficult questions are ignored. No wonder we are so miserable!

Oh yes, and on top of all of that, the one group of British citizens who can vote themselves a massive pay increase (apparently, because they are worth it) are MPs. The rest of us look on with a mixture of disbelief, contempt and anger. No wonder we are so miserable!

The trouble is that we are not miserable enough.

Only when we become so miserable that we become seriously angry will change happen.

Until then, we shall ensure that our children inherit a society in Britain that is characterised by shallowness, greed, hypocrisy and fantasy.

Perhaps our young people will grow up and be miserable enough and angry enough to do something about it. Come to think of it, perhaps the growing number of knives and guns on the streets of Britain indicates that they already are.

I hope, Mr Harris that that is an answer to your question. Our question to you, is what are you and your colleagues going to do about it?

Appendix 3

REPUBLICAN CONTRACT WITH AMERICA

As Republican Members of the House of Representatives and as citizens seeking to join that body we propose not just to change its policies, but even more important, to restore the bonds of trust between the people and their elected representatives.

That is why, in this era of official evasion and posturing, we offer instead a detailed agenda for national renewal, a written commitment with no fine print.

This year's election offers the chance, after four decades of one-party control, to bring to the House a new majority that will transform the way Congress works. That historic change would be the end of government that is too big, too intrusive, and too easy with the public's money. It can be the beginning of a Congress that respects the values and shares the faith of the American family.

Like Lincoln, our first Republican president, we intend to act "with firmness in the right, as God gives us to see the right." To restore accountability to Congress. To end its cycle of scandal and disgrace. To make us all proud again of the way free people govern themselves.

On the first day of the 104th Congress, the new Republican majority will immediately pass the following major reforms, aimed at restoring the faith and trust of the American people in their government:

- **FIRST, require all laws that apply to the rest of the country also apply equally to the Congress;**

- **SECOND, select a major, independent auditing firm to conduct a comprehensive audit of Congress for waste, fraud or abuse;**

- **THIRD, cut the number of House committees, and cut committee staff by one-third;**

- **FOURTH, limit the terms of all committee chairs;**

- **FIFTH, ban the casting of proxy votes in committee;**

- **SIXTH, require committee meetings to be open to the public;**

- **SEVENTH, require a three-fifths majority vote to pass a tax increase;**

- **EIGHTH, guarantee an honest accounting of our Federal Budget by implementing zero base-line budgeting.**

Thereafter, within the first 100 days of the 104th Congress, we shall bring to the House Floor the following bills, each to be given full and open debate, each to be given a clear and fair vote and each to be immediately available this day for public inspection and scrutiny.

1. THE FISCAL RESPONSIBILITY ACT: A balanced budget/tax limitation amendment and a legislative line-item veto to restore fiscal responsibility to an out-of-control Congress, requiring them to live under the same budget constraints as families and businesses. (Bill Text) (Description)

2. **THE TAKING BACK OUR STREETS ACT:** An anti-crime package including stronger truth-in-sentencing, "good faith" exclusionary rule exemptions, effective death penalty provisions, and cuts in social spending from this summer's "crime" bill to fund prison construction and additional law enforcement to keep people secure in their neighborhoods and kids safe in their schools. (Bill Text) (Description)

3. **THE PERSONAL RESPONSIBILITY ACT:** Discourage illegitimacy and teen pregnancy by prohibiting welfare to minor mothers and denying increased AFDC for additional children while on welfare, cut spending for welfare programs, and enact a tough two-years-and-out provision with work requirements to promote individual responsibility. (Bill Text) (Description)

4. **THE FAMILY REINFORCEMENT ACT:** Child support enforcement, tax incentives for adoption, strengthening rights of parents in their children's education, stronger child pornography laws, and an elderly dependent care tax credit to reinforce the central role of families in American society. (Bill Text) (Description)

5. **THE AMERICAN DREAM RESTORATION ACT:** A S500 per child tax credit, begin repeal of the marriage tax penalty, and creation of American Dream Savings Accounts to provide middle class tax relief. (Bill Text) (Description)

6. **THE NATIONAL SECURITY RESTORATION ACT:** No U.S. troops under U.N. command and restoration of the essential parts of our national security funding to strengthen our national defense and maintain our credibility around the world. (Bill Text) (Description)

7. **THE SENIOR CITIZENS FAIRNESS ACT:** Raise the Social Security earnings limit which currently forces seniors out of the work force, repeal the 1993 tax hikes on Social Security benefits and provide tax incentives for private long-term care insurance to let Older Americans keep more of what they have earned over the years. (Bill Text) (Description)

8. **THE JOB CREATION AND WAGE ENHANCEMENT ACT:** Small business incentives, capital gains cut and indexation, neutral cost recovery, risk assessment/cost-benefit analysis, strengthening the Regulatory Flexibility Act and unfunded mandate reform to create jobs and raise worker wages. (Bill Text) (Description)

9. **THE COMMON SENSE LEGAL REFORM ACT:** "Loser pays" laws, reasonable limits on punitive damages and reform of product liability laws to stem the endless tide of litigation. (Bill Text) (Description)

10. **THE CITIZEN LEGISLATURE ACT:** A first-ever vote on term limits to replace career politicians with citizen legislators. (Description)

Further, we will instruct the House Budget Committee

to report to the floor and we will work to enact additional budget savings, beyond the budget cuts specifically included in the legislation described above, to ensure that the Federal budget deficit will be less than it would have been without the enactment of these bills.

Respecting the judgment of our fellow citizens as we seek their mandate for reform, we hereby pledge our names to this Contract with America.

REFERENCES

'You and Your MP'   House of Commons Information

'Power to the people' (2007) Report by the Power
   Commission

The Complete Expenses Files, The Daily Telegraph
   supplement, 20 June 2009

Jury Team (www.juryteam.org)

Conservative Party manifesto)   These are available
   for the last four General

Labour Party manifesto   )   Elections on
   www.google.com and

Liberal Democrat manifesto   )   www.ask.co.uk

About the Author

The author was the Headmaster of a large London comprehensive school for 22 years and was also the seconded Head of another London school in Special Measures. In the last thirty years he has experienced, at first hand, the effects of numerous, often mutually contradictory, educational 'reforms' initiated by successive generations of politicians. Whether those 'reforms' were useful to young people, or not, the effect of constant ill-conceived fiddling was to ensure that what we do this year is different from what we did last year, and neither will be the same as what we will do next year. This is bad news for young people, as well as everyone else involved in the service.

Such experiences have lead the author to suspect that one of the qualifications required to be a politician is to have had a reality bypass.

After forty years of teaching Biology, general science and mathematics in state schools, the author is still passionate about education. He has three daughters and a son, and lives and works in Sussex.